Onward

Onward

EDITORS

Anne Ghory-Goodman
Professor Emerita
Milwaukee Institute of Art and Design
Visiting Scholar, RIT

Josh Owen
Vignelli Distinguished Professor of Design
Director, Vignelli Center for
Design Studies, RIT

FOREWORD

Michael Bierut
Partner, Pentagram

Onward

RIT Press
90 Lomb Memorial Drive
Rochester, NY 14623
http://rit.edu/press/

Cover and book design
Anne Ghory-Goodman
Bruce Ian Meader
Jason Alger
Trista Finch

ISBN 978-1-939125-81-1 (print)
ISBN 978-1-939125-82-8 (ebook)

Library of Congress
Cataloging-in-Publication Data

Names: Remington, R. Roger, honoree.
    Ghory-Goodman, Anne, 1949– editor.
    Owen, Josh, 1970– editor.
Title: Onward / editors, Anne Ghory-
    Goodman, Professor Emerita,
    Milwaukee Institute of Art and Design,
    Visiting Scholar, RIT; Josh Owen,
    Vignelli Distinguished Professor of
    Design, Director, Vignelli Center for
    Design Studies, RIT; foreword,
    Michael Bierut, Partner, Pentagram.
Other titles: Onward (RIT Press)
Description: Rochester, NY: RIT Press,
    [2021] | Summary: "Onward is a
    Festschrift with scholarly essays and
    designs published in honor of
    R. Roger Remington,
    Vignelli Distinguished Professor
    of Design Emeritus at Rochester
    Institute of Technology (RIT)

The book is a collection of
    57 contributions from 8 countries
    honoring Remington's 57 years
    of service at RIT. The Foreword is
    written by Michael Bierut, partner at
    Pentagram, and provides the historical
    context for Remington's decades of
    accomplishment and influence in the
    evolution of Modern Design."
    Provided by publisher.

Identifiers: LCCN 2021033333 (print)
    LCCN 2021033334 (ebook)
    ISBN 9781939125811 (hardcover)
    ISBN 9781939125828 (epub)
Subjects: LCSH: Remington, R. Roger.
    Graphic artists–United States.
    Rochester Institute of Technology
    Faculty
Classification: LCC NC999.4.R46 O59 2021
    (print)
    LCC NC999.4.R46 (ebook)
    DDC 740.92–dc23
    LC record available at https://
    lccn.loc.gov/2021033333
    LC ebook record available at https://
    lccn.loc.gov/2021033334

**Dedicated to
R. Roger Remington**

57 Voices
Celebrating 57 years

Rochester Institute
of Technology

Table of Contents

Photographs of R. Roger Remington
at various stages of his career
Photos courtesy of the Remington family

Saying "Roger," conjures images of a beloved, iconic design leader. Working on this book, we talked about our contributors as Chris, and Inge, and Joe, and Gene, and Rocco… dear friends, they inspired the editorial epiphany to organize Onward by first names.

R. Roger Remington: History in the Making

Michael Bierut
Partner, Pentagram

Above, left:
Michael Bierut and Massimo Vignelli
embracing at the dedication ceremony
of the Vignelli Center for Design Studies
at RIT, 16 September 2010
Photograph courtesy of Bruce Ian Meader

Above, right:
Early childhood photograph of
R. Roger Remington
Photo courtesy of the Remington family

In September 1963, the number one song in America was "My Boyfriend's Back" by the Angels; the Beatles would not release their first US single until December. The top movies were *Cleopatra*, *How the West Was Won*, and the very first James Bond film, *Dr. No*. A gallon of milk cost fifty cents and a gallon of gas cost even less, thirty cents. The average price of a new house was about twenty thousand dollars. John F. Kennedy was in his third year as president; he would not see another. In Honolulu, the month before, Barack Obama had celebrated his second birthday.

And in September 1963, R. Roger Remington arrived at his alma mater, the Rochester Institute of Technology (RIT), to teach his first class. It was figure drawing, a studio class with live models. He was twenty-seven years old and there was nowhere he would rather be.

He would remain at RIT for the next fifty-seven years, as vinyl records were replaced by cassette tapes and CDs and MP3s, through twenty-three more James Bond films, through the administrations of eleven presidents. Over that time, Roger Remington would shape the lives of thousands of students, create a new way of looking at the world of visual communication, and build a legacy that would redefine a profession. Indeed, he would make history in more ways than one.

Ah, *history*, a term that is inextricably linked with Roger Remington in the minds of so many of us. We think of history as something fixed in place, as an immutable string of facts. But history is actually no more than a series of stories to be discovered, to be shared and studied, to be understood and argued about.

It was something that Remington would have experienced firsthand as a student at RIT's School of Art and Design in the late 1950s, at a moment when the very nature of design education was changing, shifting from a focus on traditional Beaux Arts training to embrace the tenets of modernism, established at the Bauhaus but still, decades later, seeking footholds in the United States.

Remington applied to graduate school and studied at the University of Wisconsin, and then worked as a designer for several years before accepting a position as the only graphic design instructor in Montana State University at Bozeman. When he returned to RIT in 1963, it was to a place that was in the midst of radical transformation, moving from a small group of buildings in downtown Rochester to a sprawling modern campus in suburban Henrietta. Remington made his mark: he helped design the graphic identity for the relocated university, and then led the creation of the school's first graphic design department, which he would chair for seven years.

Although Remington's reputation would ultimately span disciplines, teaching was always his first love. His students, so many of whom have gone on to distinguished careers of their own, paint a vivid picture of his impact: driven and visionary, yet inspiring and fun. He won the Eisenhart Award for Outstanding Teaching, RIT's highest recognition of university-wide teaching excellence, in 1978.

It was perhaps inevitable that Roger Remington would be drawn to history as a subject and as a challenge. RIT's connection to the world of imaging and graphic reproduction, dating to longstanding relationships with some of Rochester's biggest businesses, had made it a natural home for the Cary Graphic Arts Collection, established in 1969 as a library of books, manuscripts, documents, and artifacts related to the history of graphic communication. Remington championed the growth and expansion of the collection by establishing the Cary Graphic Design Archive in 1984, obtaining the works and papers of a pantheon of design pioneers, starting with American modernist Lester Beall, and now comprising a staggering who's who of the discipline with more than forty names, including Will Burtin, Tomoko Miho, Bradbury Thompson, and Cipe Pineles. As a result, where others learn design history through books and slide lectures, RIT students can examine primary source material firsthand, and not just printed artifacts but working papers, sketches, prototypes, and models.

If the field of graphic design history has a single progenitor, it may very well be Roger Remington. He cemented this status on April 20 and 21, 1983. On those two days, five hundred designers, academics, authors, and archivists converged on the RIT campus for Coming of Age: The First Symposium on the History of Graphic Design, an event conceived, organized, and hosted by Remington. Graphic design historians were already at work—in fact, Philip Meggs's soon-to-be-canonical *A History of Graphic Design* was published that same year—but Remington's symposium brought the field's major thinkers together for the first time. It was an electrifying experience, and it effectively set a course for the explosion of scholarship that would follow.

Remington himself played a role in this scholarship with a series of books that defined American design history in the twentieth century. First came *Nine Pioneers in American Graphic Design* (1989), a survey of the work of M. F. Agha, Alexey Brodovitch, Charles Coiner, William Golden, Lester Beall, Will Burtin, Alvin Lustig, Ladislav Sutnar, and Bradbury Thompson, which examines the diverse cultural strains that combined to define the look of printed communications in this country at midcentury. Then Remington authored the definitive monographs on two of those protagonists with *Lester Beall: Trailblazer of American Graphic Design* (1996) and *Design and Science: The Life and Work of Will Burtin* (2007). Finally, his magisterial *American Modernism: Graphic Design, 1920 to 1960* (2003) examines the worldwide cultural forces that informed the modern movement in this country, and assesses that movement's influence on present-day practice.

Opposite:
All photos courtesy of the RIT Cary Graphic Design Archive, the collection of Bruce Ian Meader, and the Remington family

The most enduring evidence of Roger Remington's impact on RIT and on the world of graphic design can be found at 166 Lomb Memorial Drive, the site of the Vignelli Center for Design Studies. The legendary Massimo Vignelli had been a friend and admirer of Remington's since the 1970s; he had, in fact, delivered an often quoted keynote address at the *Coming of Age* design history symposium in 1983. ("I can't believe that for decades," Vignelli told the audience then, "graphic designers have been happy and content with simply producing and looking at pretty pictures.") Twenty years later, Vignelli and his wife and partner Lella were ready to downsize, moving from a sprawling fifteen-thousand-square-foot office on Manhattan's west side to work from home on more personal projects. This would mean finding a place for their archives, and they had only one destination in mind, RIT. But Remington quickly realized that the proposed donation—which included not just nearly five decades of papers and printed artifacts but three-dimensional models, packaging, and furniture—would overwhelm the Cary Graphic Design Archive. In response, he proposed a much bolder idea, not merely an archive, but an active center for design education, with spaces for classrooms, lectures, and exhibitions. After five years of leadership by Remington, who brilliantly shepherded the project through endless bureaucratic and financial challenges, the Vignelli Center opened in 2010, a precise, geometric jewel box designed by the Vignellis themselves.

Today, it is a globally recognized hub for education, research, collaboration, and advocacy. "The Center is like an eternal flame for design education," Remington's colleague Josh Owen has said. "And Roger has provided the fuel."

In a world too often defined by self-imposed limits, R. Roger Remington's fuel has proven to be an inexhaustible resource. Over the course of an astounding six decades, he has worked tirelessly to examine and celebrate the past while securing a future for generations of designers and design enthusiasts yet unborn. For as monumental as it may seem today, his influence has only just begun. Roger Remington still has a lot of history to make.

Michael Bierut

Opposite, left to right, top to bottom: First RIT Identity designed by Roger Remington; Remington in his office and teaching students; American Modernism Graphic Design 1920 to 1960, *by Roger Remington, Laurence King, London 2003;* The First Symposium on the History of Graphic Design, *publication cover; RIT Cary Graphic Design Archive logotype and interior; Rural Electrification Association poster design by Lester Beall, 1937; Go Out, Woman's Day magazine, ad design by Gene Federico, 1953; Lella and Massimo Vignelli and Roger Remington, at RIT's Vignelli Center for Design Studies dedication, 2010*

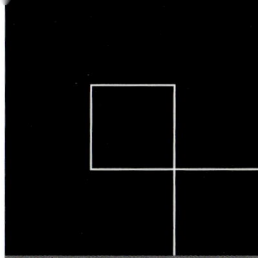

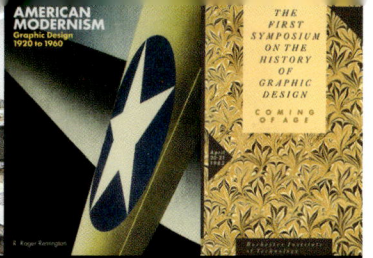

David C. Munson Jr.
RIT President

Ellen Granberg
RIT Provost and Senior Vice President
for Academic Affairs

Message from the President and the Provost

R. Roger Remington has served as the face of design at RIT for nearly six decades, raising the profile of the College of Art and Design and the university in the design world to new heights. He has transformed the university into an international archival resource for design while earning many of the industry's most distinguished accolades along the way.

A titan in the field of design both at RIT—through his efforts that established design as a pillar of our university—and in the broader world of design, Roger is rightly recognized as a world-class historian, scholar, author, and designer at large.

He was first introduced to RIT back in the 1950s, when he was an art and design student. And it was Stanley Witmeyer, the head of the School of Art and Design in the early 1960s, who invited Roger back to RIT to teach as we were building the new campus in Henrietta.

We are so fortunate that he did.

Roger helped build the first graphic design department while he began to make a significant impact on students in the classroom. He received the Eisenhart Award for Outstanding Teaching—RIT's highest recognition of teaching excellence—in 1978.

Renowned worldwide for his critical interests in design studies, research, writing, and graphic design practice, Roger has been engaged in the research, interpretation, and preservation of the history of graphic design since the early 1980s.

He was the leading catalyst in establishing RIT's Cary Graphic Design Archive, which now features more than forty-five collections of modernist American graphic design pioneers. The crown jewel of his archival efforts, the Vignelli Center for Design Studies, houses the archive of the late distinguished designers Massimo and Lella Vignelli, whose graphic and product designs are icons of international design.

At the time of the center's dedication, Massimo Vignelli said the project would never have been built without Roger, whom the late designer called the center's soul and who made the archive a teaching instrument and a formidable legacy to RIT. Due in large part to Roger's tireless work, the Vignelli Center for Design Studies now serves as an invaluable resource to our students, our faculty, and design scholars around the globe.

Through these accomplishments and so many more, Roger leaves an indelible mark on the university—and the design industry at large. His wonderful legacy will benefit the university, and the design world, for years to come.

David C. Munson Jr.
RIT President

Ellen Granberg
RIT Provost and Senior Vice President
for Academic Affairs

Left:
Vignelli Center for Design Studies at RIT

Below:
Front row: Valentina Vignelli,
Massimo and Lella Vignelli,
Lady Helen Hamlyn, R. Roger Remington
Dedication 16 September 2010
Vignelli Center for Design Studies

Photos this page by Elizabeth Lamark
courtesy Vignelli Center archives

Message from the Dean
R. Roger Remington
in Brief

Todd Jokl
Dean, College of Art and Design
Rochester Institute of Technology

Opposite:
Illustration of R. Roger Remington
by Industrial Design Professor
Dan Harel, based on a photograph by
Elizabeth Lamark, 2014

Occasionally... rarely, there are people we encounter in academia or our professional fields who are known across the spectrum because of their ingenuity, their generosity, and the "family tree" to which we can connect so many ideas and practitioners. For those of us who are lucky enough to study under or work with such a person, we appreciate the rarity of such an experience and we cherish the bond created among multiple generations of professionals, scholars, and affiliated peers.
For me and my own undergraduate studies, the late art and architecture critic and historian, Vincent Scully, was such a person.

For Rochester Institute of Technology (RIT) and its generations of students in the fields of design, and for professionals across the design disciplines, R. Roger Remington is the figure who transcends our program and binds us together with common questions and statements of affirmation like "Oh! You studied/worked with Roger, too?!" and "Roger's class changed my life." I have been tasked with the simplest of challenges: celebrate Mr. Remington's achievements and meaningfulness to the field of design education in a brief submission for this Festschrift. Oh, really?

R. Roger Remington has watched over the graphic design curriculum at RIT since 1963. Perhaps his most significant contribution to our curriculum, our students, and the field more broadly, is his groundbreaking work in the field of design history. To say that Roger's work in design history is "seminal" is an understatement. As evidenced through the meaningful and significant contributors in this Festschrift, Roger has led and engaged in conversations with the most influential designers and design thinking in modern and contemporary practice. He has steadfastly brought meaning to the lineage of design work, connecting historical with modern with contemporary, and locating it all within the lexicon, the lingua franca, of design vocabulary.

His publication and presentation record is a breadcrumb trail of innovative and inventive thinking, critique, and theory about the most practical elements as well as abstract ideas in design over the past six decades.

Here at home, in addition to being a beloved teacher for some fifty-seven years, he has led transformative initiatives that have placed RIT at a central point in design studies and history. Two such examples are his work as a champion of RIT's Cary Graphic Arts Collection and, the bookend to his storied career, the Vignelli Center for Design Studies— a celebration of not only the Vignellis' design principles but the language of design and the multiple collections representing the ideas and ideals of design. Ultimately, as Roger will avow, the most important and lasting mission of both the Cary Graphic Arts Collection and the Vignelli Center for Design Studies is the accessibility they provide to students, professionals, and the public as resources for hands-on research. These, alone, are astonishing legacies that will inform future designers at RIT and around the world.

In the end, the challenge is not describing the accolades of such a transformative figure within the limits of an arbitrary word count. The challenge is asking (and answering), How does one honor the career of an educator, a colleague, a mentor, and an intellectual such as R. Roger Remington?

I believe the answer is that we carry forward the ideas and ideals R. Roger Remington has introduced to the world. We carry forward with the passion and inspiration he has breathed into the minds of so many young design students and mature professionals alike. We carry forward with the belief that design can continue to make the world a better place. For we know that R. Roger Remington, through his life's work, has made design, designers, and the world a much better place.

Todd Jokl
Dean, College of Art and Design
Rochester Institute of Technology

Anne Ghory-Goodman
Josh Owen

Message from the Editors

Why a Festschrift?
Why Onward?

R. Roger Remington has been a professor at Rochester Institute of Technology for fifty-seven years. A collection of writings, a Festschrift, published to honor his life as a designer, educator and scholar, is a perfect tribute. It includes essays and visual messages from 57 contributors from 8 countries who are representative of the scores of people he touched.

Roger believes in the relevance of history. He has taught about it, he writes about it, and he acts on his beliefs. He created the first symposium on the History of Graphic Design at RIT. He helped establish the Cary Graphic Design Archive, and he made the Vignelli Center for Design Studies the centerpiece of his legacy.

Roger is a historian and a futurist. He constantly suggests new ways of using archives. He maintains a long list of people he wants to invite to speak. He has new books to write on his desk.

He studies the past but lives looking ahead. He signs his emails, "ONWARD". This book is a part of RIT's celebration of R. Roger Remington, the Vignelli Distinguished Professor of Design. It exists despite the challenges of the COVID-19 pandemic and through the generosity of the many contributors who made the content so rich; with thanks to RIT Graphic Design Professor Emeritus Bruce Ian Meader, RIT Graphic Design Alumna Trista Finch and Kendall College of Art and Design Graphic Design Professor Jason Alger for helping us to craft this at the highest level. We are also indebted to RIT's President, Provost and Dean of the College of Art and Design for their support and to the RIT Press for their shared vision of a book that will honor the past and be meaningful in the future.

This book includes only a small, representative sample of Roger's colleagues and accomplishments. Roger's legacy continues to be written by his distinguished colleagues at RIT and the generations he has nurtured around the world.

Onward.

Anne Ghory-Goodman
Professor Emerita
Milwaukee Institute of Art and Design
Visiting Scholar, RIT

Josh Owen
Vignelli Distinguished Professor of Design
Director, Vignelli Center for Design Studies, RIT

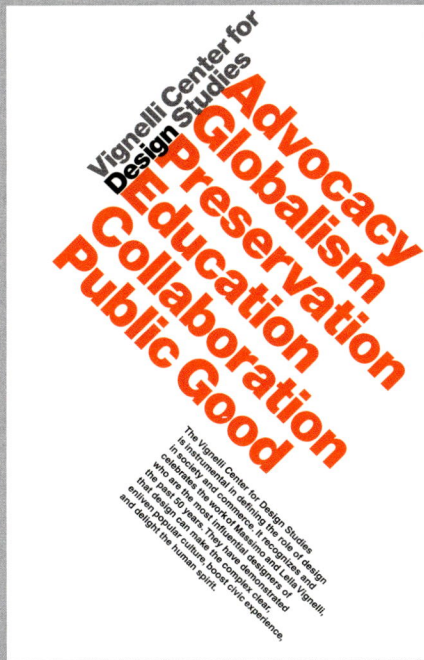

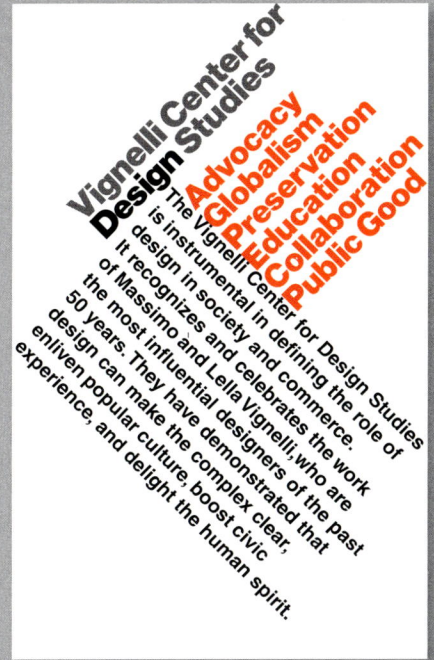

Poster series
The six goals in the Mission Statement of
the Vignelli Center for Design Studies
Designed by R. Roger Remington and
Bruce Ian Meader

Festschrift.
It's not a word
I know offhand.

Aaris Sherin
Professor of Graphic Design
St. John's University

But that's not unusual if it's associated with R. Roger Remington. For nearly twenty years, my connection with Roger, his work, and his life mission has kept me on my toes and prompted me to keep stretching to find the next horizon in design research, history, and scholarship.

As educators, our impact is often felt as more of a continuum than in a single moment. Such is the case with Roger Remington. He spent years delving into the work and lives of modernist designers in the US, and these endeavors are where the discipline will probably say he has had the greatest impact. Roger's work as a design historian and writer has undoubtedly helped reshape the way we think about graphic design, but that's only part of the story.

Today, a Sunday, I emailed back and forth with several students who are struggling to find their footing as they approach new design projects. As I ruminated on what I could contribute to this Festschrift, and was thankful that no prerequisite to pronounce the word came with the invitation, I spent time editing a junior faculty member's first efforts at writing a book review. Later in the day, I'll talk to a colleague about a writing workshop for design educators and discuss the possibility of reviving a defunct academic journal with scholars across two continents. All these activities are tied directly or indirectly to my time studying with and working as a graduate assistant for Roger.

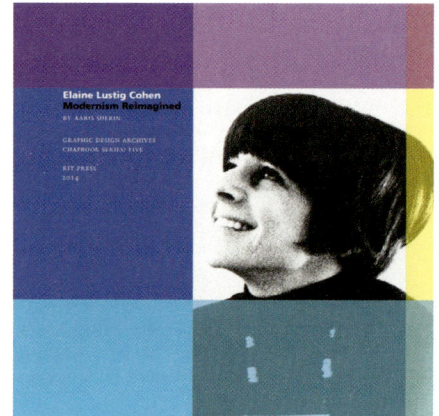

Elaine Lustig Cohen: Modernism Reimagined, *by Aaris Sherin,*
RIT Press, 2014
Design by Bruce Ian Meader

There's no manual on how to make an impact in graphic design. And that's probably because, between all his other projects, Roger just never found time to write one. What he did do is to model a life spent in and for design. This is design with a capital D. It's more than just a job or the choice to wear cool glasses and trendy shoes. Roger showed me that it is possible, and even preferable, to immerse oneself in design the way a musician makes practice and performance a part of her everyday life.

As an RIT graduate student, I arrived with a keen interest in research and history. I left with a lifelong passion for education and for design writing and scholarship. But more importantly, I graduated with the understanding that I was part of a tradition where design could be at the center of a creative life. First as Roger's graduate assistant and later, briefly, on a design-related expedition after graduation, I witnessed Roger's engagement with scholars and students both in the US and in Europe, and with curators and famous designers I had previously only read about in books. From Roger I learned that sometimes it's worth sleeping on a hard wooden floor to discover how design is taught on another continent. I learned the value of conducting extensive research before one begins a project, and through his own work, Roger showed me the joys and frustrations of working with original source material.

Roger and I don't talk on the phone or write back and forth. Our careers and lives have taken somewhat different paths and are distinctly our own. We don't even exchange holiday cards. After all, so many holiday cards are poorly designed and we wouldn't want to add to the plethora of crappy visuals in the world. But we are still connected and are an active part of a small circle of people dedicated to design education, to writing, and to research. And we continue to follow each other's work through projects each spends time on—sending copies of newly published books to each other when they are released and meeting at exhibitions or for diner pancakes in the city. The generosity of spirit that I felt as a newly enrolled graduate student is just as strong today as it was twenty years ago.

It's possible that I would still see myself as writer and scholar even if I had never met or worked with Roger. Education was a calling, and regardless of whether I had ended up at RIT, I would probably still teach design. But my work with and connection to Roger made doing the things that have brought form and structure to my life easier.

Mentors and mentorship come in many forms. Roger didn't find me publishers or even edit my writing. Over the years, we've spent countless hours talking about education, but he didn't "teach" me to be a good teacher. Instead he led by example. He epitomizes what a life for and in design could look like. He modeled how to continue to be a vital and engaged educator and scholar decades after receiving tenure. And he showed me how taking an active interest in a newer or younger faculty person's work can positively impact their entire career. These are the things I internalized because of the time I spent with Roger, and I hope I can model these same values to a new generation of design faculty.

It's tempting to write about this moment being the end of a great and truly influential career. I could say that when he retires, Roger will leave enormous shoes to fill. But come on… this is Roger Remington we're talking about. Roger may be retiring from RIT, but he isn't retiring from design. I am confident that his work and his life in design will continue and that Roger will keep leading by example.

Roger Remington
Presentation

Albert Paley
Sculptor, Author, Educator

I commend Roger Remington's commitment to teaching, education, scholarship, and the professionalism that he has brought to the field of design. It was instrumental in the evolution and development of various skills and disciplines that were to become the foundation and structure of the design program.

Professionally, his activities and engagement have not only influenced the cultural dimension of the art and design programs at RIT, but have also had national and international influence and impact. Lectures, conferences, and various forums in which he has contributed internationally aided in the understanding of the design process and the related educational structure of those disciplines. His international contributions and networking enhanced not only

the design programs at RIT but the broader field of design as well. Scholarship and the responsibility to education extended into his appreciation of other practitioners within the field of design. Remington was responsible for creating a repository for the archives of various designers at RIT— not just for individual legacy but as a valuable information database for study. This commitment, embraced by the university, ultimately resulted in the establishment of the Vignelli Center, bringing in these archives and developing the programs... as well as the physical space for the center. This has created the format for the important future role that RIT will play in this area of study, in large part because of Remington's leadership, discipline, and commitment to education.

The most valuable accolade to be bestowed upon a colleague is one of admiration and respect. As a colleague, and through a friendship that has developed over these many years, I have been pleased to have the opportunity to experience the enrichment that Roger has offered. Due to his many activities, so many faculty and students have been enriched—my respect and admiration.

What a valuable contribution Roger Remington has afforded RIT with his many years of commitment, and with the living legacy of those activities embodied in the Vignelli Center for Design Studies.

Opposite, left:
A Conversation: Albert Paley and
R. Roger Remington
Memorial Art Gallery, 2019
Photo by Suzanne Remington

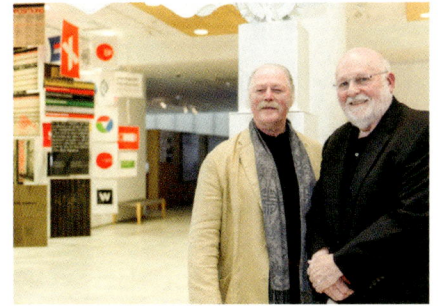

Above:
Albert Paley and R. Roger Remington
at the Vignelli Center for Design Studies
Photo by Suzanne Remington

Beneath
the Surface

Anne Ghory-Goodman
Photographer, Designer, Educator
Professor Emerita
Milwaukee Institute of Art and Design
Visiting Scholar, RIT

Looking superficially is not seeing. Asking how and why takes us to greater depths. By discovering and sharing patterns, historians help us see the past come alive beneath the present's surface.

The best historians are contextual raconteurs. Reveling in the backstories they share, we learn to separate background and foreground. Historians peer through a faceted lens at people and events, then paint a revealing picture. Peeling away layers, they make intentions visible. They dive deeply, then reemerge with their insights.

Inquisitive historians collect and examine artifacts. They visit significant sites. They lecture around the world and interview people who were central (or tangential) to events. Historians delight in sharing their discoveries. At best, they reveal what we can learn by examining the world from many viewpoints. (At worst, they color facts to support biased views.)

Coming of Age: The First Symposium on the History of Graphic Design at RIT was attended by five hundred luminaries, practitioners, educators, and authors who knew they were participating in something extraordinary—making the history of graphic design relevant and enhancing the perception of graphic design as a profession. Conceived by Roger Remington, the conference catapulted him to a lifelong role as modern design's de facto public champion.

Roger believed in the efficacy of archives to catalyze scholarship, inspire innovative teaching, and encourage hands-on examination of legendary work.

Massimo Vignelli famously proclaimed, "Good design is timeless." It takes a design historian to help us see how this can be so.

Opposite:
A swimming pool in Havana, Cuba, appears colorful, nuanced, and faceted beneath the surface in a city burdened and illuminated by its patina of history. Photo collage by Anne Ghory-Goodman reflecting the influence of Norman Ives

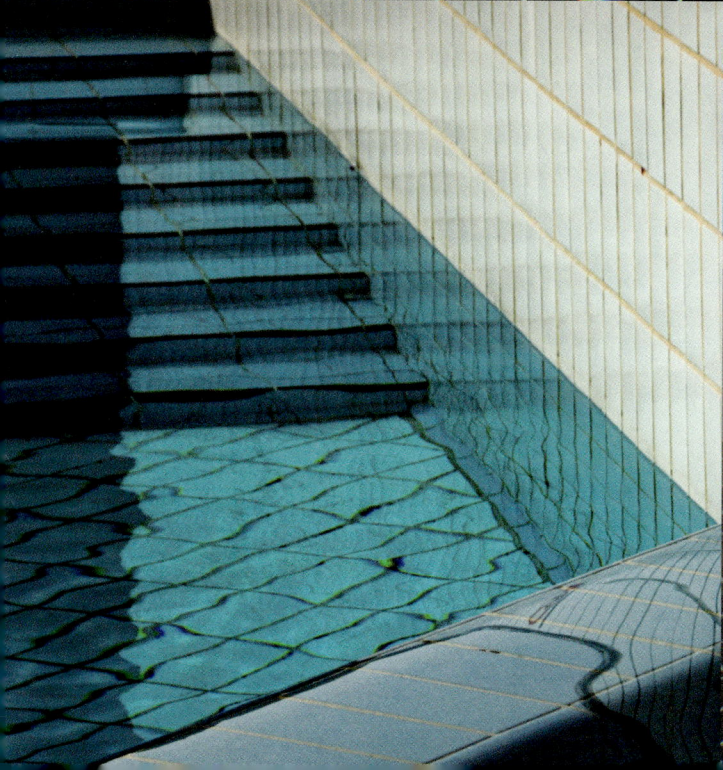

Armando Milani
Graphic Designer, Author, Educator

To Roger

Remington

Above:
Cineclub Brera
from No Words Posters, *RIT Press, 2015*
Foreword by R. Roger Remington
Poster design, Armando Milani, 1975

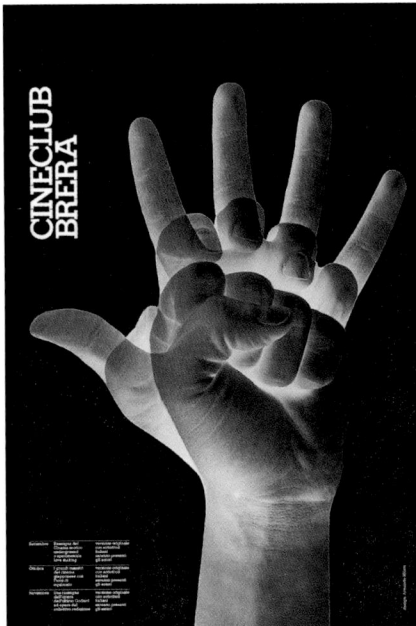

Roger was introduced to me by Massimo Vignelli in New York in 1998. They were planning the construction of the Vignelli Center building at Rochester Institute of Technology.

Roger had the difficult task of mediating between the multitude of requests by the Vignellis and the limits set by the architects and the various sponsors of the work.

Thanks also to Roger, the Vignelli Center was inaugurated with great success in 2010.

The most prestigious pieces of American graphic designers are kept there, in addition to the complete production by Massimo and Lella Vignelli. I am very grateful to Roger because, on that occasion, he organized an exhibition of my works in the exhibition space of the Vignelli Center.

Then, together with Roger and Massimo, we organized some graphic design workshops in my mill in Provence, in the South of France, for international students who are still grateful for this experience. I remember that, when we were at my mill, we shared not only a great passion for graphics, but also appreciation for certain French rosé wines.

Roger generously wrote two introductions for my books, *No Words Posters* and *Armando Milani Graphic Adventure.*

Many times I was his guest in his beautiful home in Rochester, and I remember the lavender fragrance of the sheets prepared for me by his lovely wife Suzanne. I will never forget their kindness and generosity.

Armando Milani

*Suzanne and R. Roger
Remington, Cynthia and
Armando Milani, Lella
and Massimo Vignelli,
Master Designer
Workshop, 2011
Provence, France
Photo courtesy of
Armando Milani*

Thanks
Roger.

Bill Bonnell
Designer, Artist, Novelist

Every profession needs great practitioners and great educators. Graphic Design has had many of both. But it also needs a history. Over the last forty years that has begun to emerge. Books have been written, articles published, and the whole idea of a graphic design history has taken root. When I studied in the sixties, design history was never mentioned.

What Roger has done is make graphic design history concrete. While it's nice to see a reproduction in a book, it is nothing like seeing the real thing, and sensing the physicality and scale of even two-dimensional examples. Seeing the colors true and seeing the actual paper changes everything. It's the same difference between an art reproduction and a real painting.

Roger meeting Massimo was a match made in heaven. Massimo never doubted his own greatness to be sure, but he also understood history and knew that his work, and the work of others should be preserved as part of a continuum. And Roger had the intellect and skills to actually accomplish it.

And in addition to all this Roger has helped educate several generations of designers who will hopefully make this world a better place. The world certainly needs it.

I wish Roger a great retirement, but something tells me there may be a third act.

Bill Bonnell
Norwalk, Connecticut, 2020
Thanks

Opposite:
Typographic Illustration, 2020
Design by Bill Bonnell

ROGER REMINGTON MADE HISTORY IMPORTANT

Bruce Ian Meader
Graphic Design Educator
RIT Colleague
Professor Emeritus

Advocacy: Getting Religion

For twenty-six years R. Roger Remington was my colleague in graphic design at RIT. We would often say that every day is a battle against the forces of mediocrity. To this day, we share a deep and abiding love for design that is beautiful and, most importantly, functions on a high level to improve the quality of people's lives. Roger is my best friend.

Among his many words of wisdom, Roger has frequently described the time when a person (most often a student) finally had a eureka moment and understood some aspect of design: Roger would say they "got religion."

Over his fifty-seven years as a design historian and educator, Roger has had so many disciples who are beneficiaries of his teaching, and many of them have gone on to give others "religion." Roger is a beacon in his advocacy for good design. It is a major contribution he has given the world.

An extension of this advocacy manifests itself through Roger's lifelong collection of the work of prominent designers. Early on, Roger made it his business to assemble over forty complete lifework archives of important design pioneers. This collection is one of the crown jewels at RIT: the Cary Graphic Design Archive and, now celebrating its tenth year, the Vignelli Center for Design Studies.

Students at most schools, if they are lucky, see some of this important design work as postage-stamp-sized images projected on a screen. At RIT, students visit the Graphic Design Archive and can actually hold early color sketches of Lester Beall's Rural Electrification Administration posters. This intimate contact resource enables students to have a profound and lasting experience, one that ensures a deeper understanding of the principles and issues of effective design.

Legions of educators, students, and practitioners have made the pilgrimage to RIT to study these amazing resources. And most recently, people have come to the Vignelli Center for Design Studies to observe and study the critical work in this magnificent collection. Here again, it's not just a final artifact that can be seen but often a range of early sketches and prototypes that reveal the details and significance of the design process. It is impossible to overstate the importance of this kind of advocacy, which spreads the word far and wide to so many. We all owe Roger a debt of gratitude for his years of advocating essential, effective, and timeless design. While Roger Remington is retiring after his extraordinary teaching career, his legacy will live on forever so the efficacy of good design will be there for others to witness, digest, and absorb.

And that is the gospel truth!

Lester Beall
Space, Time & Content
BY R. ROGER REMINGTON

GRAPHIC DESIGN ARCHIVES
CHAPBOOK SERIES: ONE

RIT
CARY GRAPHIC ARTS PRESS
2003

Cipe Pineles
Two Remembrances
BY ESTELLE ELLIS
AND CAROL BURTIN FLOW

GRAPHIC DESIGN ARCHIVES
CHAPBOOK SERIES: TWO

RIT
CARY GRAPHIC ARTS PRESS
2004

Purity of Aim:
The Book Jacket Designs
of Alvin Lustig
BY NED DREW
AND PAUL STERNBERGER

GRAPHIC DESIGN ARCHIVES
CHAPBOOK SERIES: FOUR

RIT
CARY GRAPHIC ARTS PRESS
2010

RELIGION

ENLIGHTEN

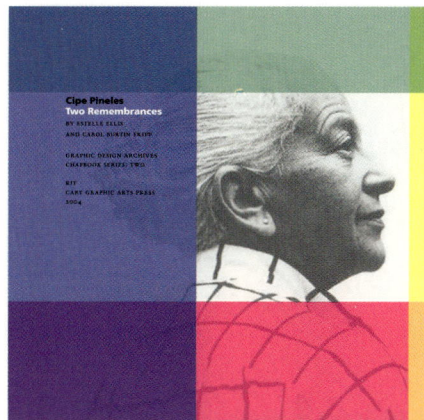

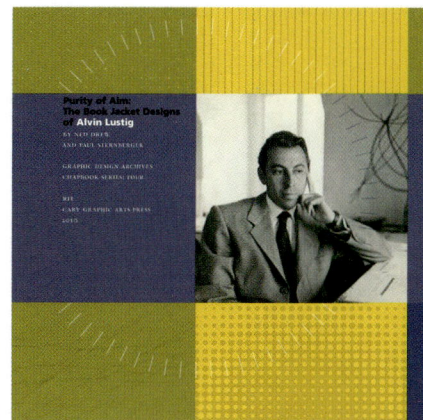

Left:
Sophomore type student Greg Vottero designed facing compositions using excerpts from the famous Scopes Trial, in which trial lawyer Clarence Darrow defended biology teacher John Scopes's right to teach evolution against the prosecutor, William Jennings Bryan. The letters R (organic) and E (geometric) face back-to-back, to convey the dichotomy of this argument. This kind of problem, focused on meaning and form, continues to be a shared passion for Roger and me.

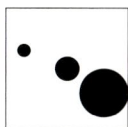

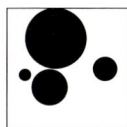

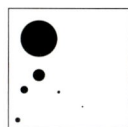

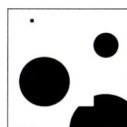

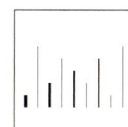

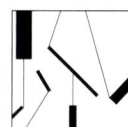

Yingshan Wu

These are fundamental formal exercises in which students explore interval, contrast, proportion, implied edge, and tension.

Evgenia Tranevskaya

While they are elementary, I taught these at the undergraduate and graduate levels to ensure all students get this exposure.

Yingshan Wu

Roger and I believe a deep understanding of this formalism is essential to making elegant, powerful, and timeless design.

Bruno Monguzzi
Educator and Designer

Corso universitario in medicina
d'urgenza e di catastrofe
Universitärer Kurs in Notfall-
und Katastrophenmedizin
(University Course in Emergency
and Catastrophe Medicine)
Poster, 63 x 42 cm, 1991 (detail)
Photographer unknown
Design by Bruno Monguzzi

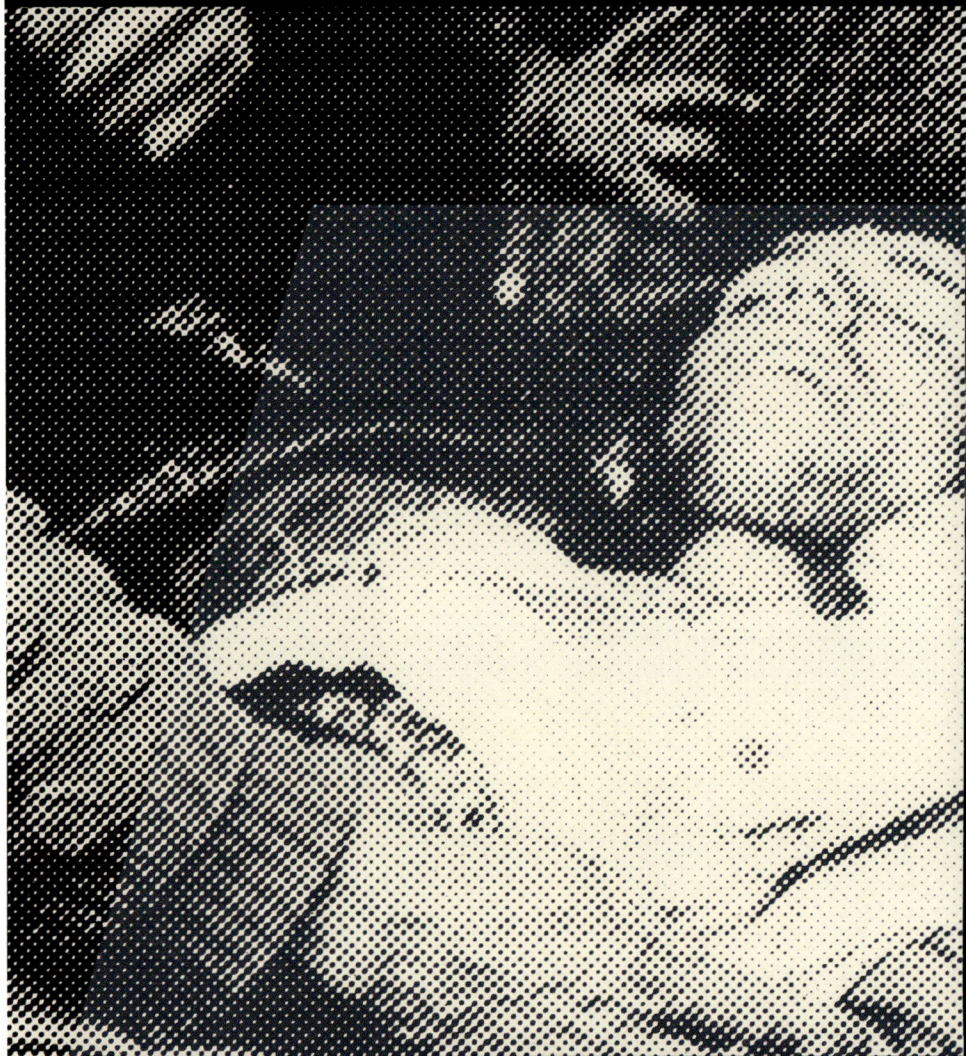

per   candidati medici
        medici
        personale sanitario
        samaritani
    specialisti e interessati
    nel pronto soccorso
    salvataggio

Bellinzona
Castel Grande
29. 30. 31. Agosto
August 1991

Corso universitario in

d' medicina

urgenza

e di catastrofe

Universitärer Kurs in

und Notfall

Katas

strophen

medizin

Spreading the Design Gospel

Burton Kramer
CM, OOnt, DDes (Hon)
RCA, AGI, FGDC, RGD
MFA (Yale), BSc

I arrived in Toronto in the fall of 1965, with my Swiss wife and baby daughter, after two and a half years as chief designer of a Swiss advertising agency in Zurich, to be design director of the Toronto office of a Canadian firm with offices in three cities.

I soon discovered that I could count on my fingers the Canadian designers doing work that I could relate to. The International Style was practiced by a very small group, many of them with Swiss or German backgrounds and/or training.

For one year I worked at top speed designing many graphic solutions for Expo 67.

As the Expo creative project ended, I was "let go" but soon found employment at Clairtone Sound Corp. as Corporate Design Director. The work I did there was published in *Idea* magazine, Tokyo.

A year later, in the fall of 1967, I started my own office, with the Royal Ontario Museum as a sustaining client. A corporate identity program for Channel 19, the *Ontario Educational Communications Authority*, a magazine for the Ontario Institute for Studies in Education, and graphics for the new planetarium soon followed. I began teaching corporate identity design (part-time) at Ontario College of Art, which continued for twenty-one years.

I cannot congratulate Roger enough on his amazing fifty-seven years of teaching at RIT and the long-lasting influence he has, and will continue to have, on his students and colleagues.

In 1974, my office won the contract to design a new bilingual visual identity for the Canadian Broadcasting Corporation (CBC) and Radio Canada International. I became one of the first Canadian members of AGI.

It was around this time that I first met Roger, and we seemed to have a great deal in common. I was invited to RIT as Designer in Residence and was asked to be a member of the local Art Direction Design exhibition.

In 2010 to 2011, Roger was kind enough to write the introduction to a comprehensive book on my work, edited by Greg Durrell, titled *Burton Kramer/Identities, A Half Century of Graphic Design/1958–2008*.

Roger and I kept in contact. I began painting lyrical, colorist, geometry-based imagery. Following my retirement from design and shows in Toronto galleries, a major show of my paintings was organized at the RIT University Gallery in 2012. We will never forget the memorable dinner with Roger, Suzanne, our son, and daughter at the Dinosaur Bar-B-Que restaurant in Rochester. Fantastic!

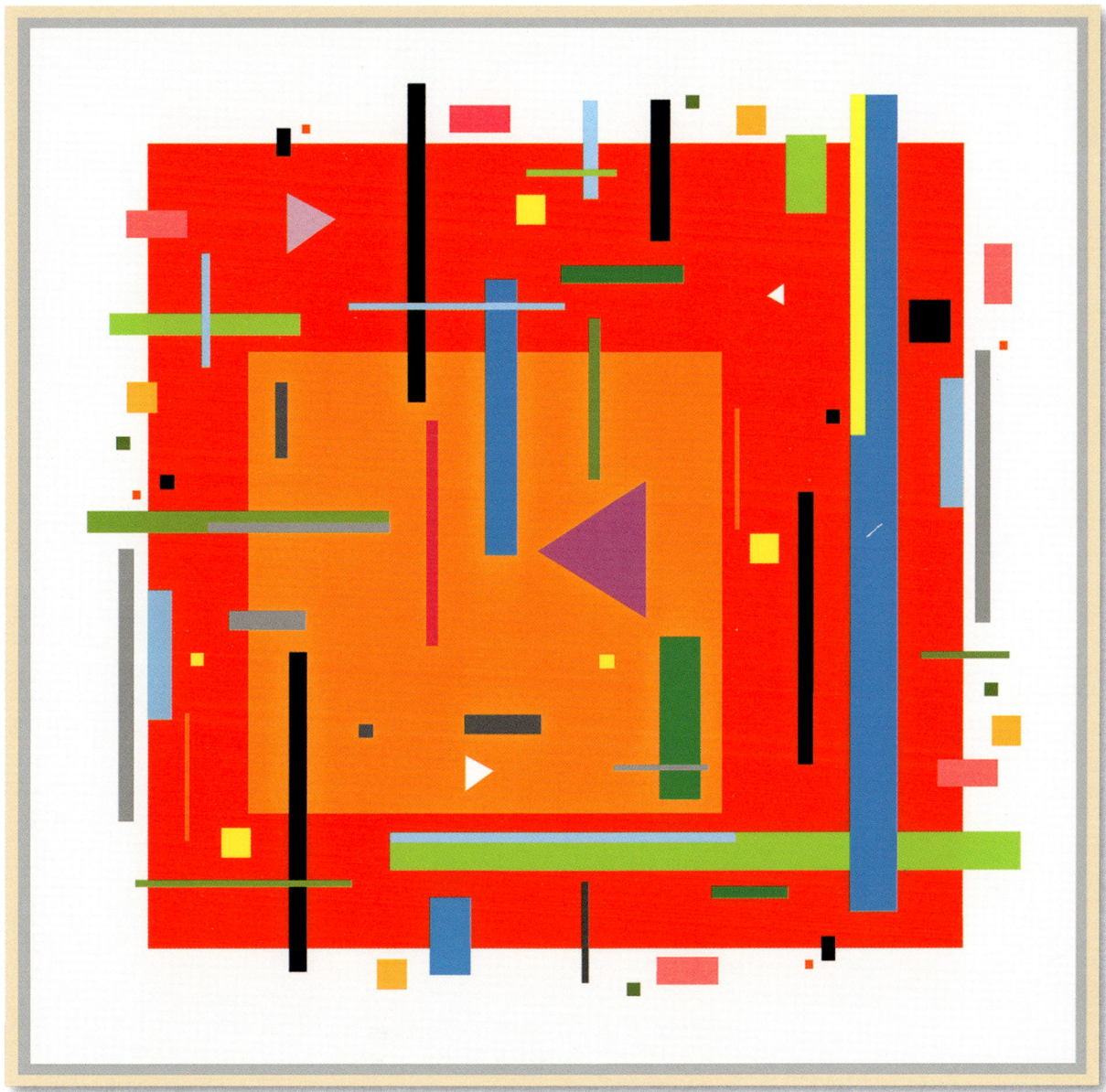

Bourée 2A4A, 2007,
acrylic on canvas, 42 x 42 inches
Design by Burton Kramer

Point,
Line,
and Shape

Carol Fillip
RIT Graduate, Educator, Designer

The first time I met Roger was in 2002, and I had just started graduate school at RIT. There was a reception in Booth 3310 with the faculty and incoming graduate students. Roger was making his rounds throughout the room when he stopped and introduced himself to me. The first thing out of my mouth after he told me he was Roger Remington was, "I know your name from my design books!" Naturally that caught his attention. I couldn't help but think that it was going to be a really good two years. Little did I know, it was the start of a lasting friendship.

Several years after graduate school, I started a three-year visiting position at RIT. I was placed with Roger as his office mate. What a thrill that was. Our shared passion for teaching the fundamental elements of graphic design through point, line, and shape gave us a great deal to talk about.

I was thankful that I could always count on Roger to have a lengthy conversation with me about line intervals, Gestalt, design systems, or graphic design education.

Roger taught various classes on the graduate and undergraduate level. He believed it was vitally important to have a senior faculty member teaching one of our foundational courses, and he took the lead on the Elements of Graphic Design class. At that time, he and I taught all the Elements courses. He generously shared his projects and handouts with me. The class was very well developed—one project plausibly leading to the next. We started with simple dots, moved to intervals, then shapes, and beyond. Despite his greater experience, he welcomed my ideas for expanding the projects and making improvements.

It was inspiring to sit and look through books with Roger and talk about the work, whether it was Karl Gerstner's *Designing Programmes* or Armin Hofmann's *Graphic Design Manual*. Very often he would suggest some of his books for me to read, and he always let me borrow them. I remember on one occasion he lent me a book for a class I was teaching, and as with many of his books, I tried to purchase a copy for myself. When I realized a copy would cost nine hundred dollars on Amazon, I carefully packed it back up and took it immediately back to the office.

Roger kept many of the cherished items that he had collected over the years in the office we shared. He knew I had a love for teaching color theory in practice. One day, when we were having our typical noodle soup lunch in the office, he pulled off the shelf a hardcover gray cloth portfolio that was approximately

15" x 20." Inside was a collection of silk-screen prints articulating Josef Albers's color theories. I couldn't believe my eyes. This amazing artifact was sitting on the shelf, right there in our office! Roger casually showed me these stunning Albers prints as I stood in wonder asking questions about where he had obtained such a treasure.

Roger has always been so kind and generous to me with his time, resources, knowledge, support, and friendship. He has been an incredible mentor. He has graciously shared his projects, files, videos, books, and insightfulness. To this day, any time I email Roger, he replies almost immediately. Any time I ask him to be a special guest in my class, he is there when I need him.

I frequently talk about Roger with my students, and any time I see an impressive set of intervals, an interesting figure-ground relationship, a beautifully resolved curve, or a multistable image, I think of Roger. I'm certain his legacy will be indelibly etched in my memory, and in the future achievements of each of the students he has inspired.

All images from the personal collection of Carol Fillip

Forging Connections to Preserve the Past and Influence the Future

Chris Bailey
RIT Graduate
President and CEO
Bailey Brand Consulting

I first heard about Roger during my junior year as a photography major at RIT. I was very envious of the "design thinking" that was being taught in his classes (my friends referred to him as Obi-Wan Kenobi). Curricula were rigidly siloed during that era, so crossing the border into the design school was somewhat frowned upon—and Roger was in high demand, with the majority of his time generously spent with the students in his classes.

My role as the student coordinator for the William A. Reedy Memorial Lectures finally provided an opportunity for introduction. Funded by Eastman Kodak, the series was the concept of Max Lomont (Vice President of Global Design for the Quaker Oats Company), Rudy Muller (JRM Media), and Vince Lisanti (Lisanti Inc.).

The Vignelli Center for Design Studies ribbon-cutting ceremony, 2010.
Left-to-right: RIT President Bill Destler, Lady Helen Hamlyn, Lella Vignelli, Roger Remington, Armando Milani, Massimo Vignelli
Photo by Elizabeth Lamark

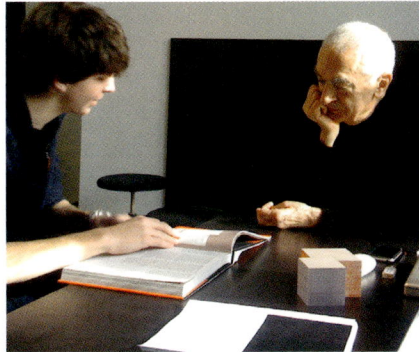

Tim Bailey with Massimo Vignelli, 2009
Photo by Chris Bailey

Max, Rudy, and Vince were well-connected professionals who had the ability to bring big names to RIT, such as Henry Wolf, Mort Goldsholl, and Annie Leibovitz, to name a few. When Roger got wind that Saul Bass was coming to campus and that I was acting as his handler, I found my "in" to become part of Roger's universe.

Many of my professors thought I spent too much time on the Reedy lecture series. However, Roger encouraged me to learn as much as possible about the world outside of school. That was great advice, as I went on to work for both Rudy and Vince in New York, and Max became a client once I started my own company.

Following graduation, I collaborated with Roger to produce an event called *The Business Edge* in conjunction with the Corporate Design Foundation; and Roger invited me to sit on the Advisory Board of the School of Design.

Roger has always demonstrated an uncanny ability to tap into his vast network of friends and professional acquaintances to achieve amazing things. The Vignelli Center for Design Studies is the pinnacle of his storied life's journey. That anyone could convince Massimo and so many other design legends to part with their archives is a true testament to his sincerity and purpose. I feel very fortunate that Roger invited me into the team that would work together to make the Vignelli Center dream a reality.

Over the years, Roger has kindly kept our firm in mind and connected us with some excellent new talent. Most notable is Gary LaCroix, who is now one of our Associate Creative Directors and has been a major part of our organization for over twenty years. Roger has also visited on many occasions to help celebrate some of the milestones along our more than thirty-five-year journey.

Roger has come to refer to me as his "best supporting alum," a badge I wear with honor. I am very lucky to have had the opportunity to get to know him when I was a student and even luckier to be able to call him a true friend of many, many years.

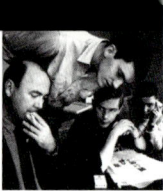

An Education

Chris and Esther Pullman
Chris Pullman
Designer, Painter, Teacher

Esther Pullman
Designer, Photographer

Roger: your 2015 exhibition of the striking work by Norman Ives was emblematic of your pioneering efforts, sustained over decades of research, writing and collecting, to endow design with its own history. We were lucky enough to have Norman as our teacher at Yale. That memorable in-person education has been enriched for us and countless other students over the years by an essential string of R. R. books and beautifully curated exhibits, as well as the trust and support you earned from your university for the meticulous archive of our profession that you have created. Thank you.

Above:
Chris Pullman in 1964, absorbing a critique by Norman Ives with classmates Arthur Congdon and Dick Ritter
Photo by Esther Pullman, 1964

Right:
Esther Pullman enjoying the exhibit Norman Ives: Constructions and Reconstructions, RIT, 2015
Photo by Chris Pullman, 2015

34

Championing a Humanitarian Vision of Design

Dan Harel
Adjunct Professor of Industrial Design
College of Art and Design, IdeaLab
Lead and Adviser, Simone Center for
Innovation and Entrepreneurship, RIT

How a single conference inspired design education and advanced a stronger connection between industry and academia

In 2014, Roger Remington, the Director of the Vignelli Center for Design Studies here at RIT, initiated the *Medicine+Design Healthcare and Wellness* Conference. As a contributor and presenter at that conference, I had the opportunity to witness his dedication to educational leadership, and through that, his commitment to public betterment.

The conference was intended as a global educational initiative to bring five international design programs together to collaborate, create, and present innovative and inclusive solutions to challenges relating to health and wellness. The participating institutions included the Vignelli Center for Design Studies at RIT, the Helen Hamlyn Centre for Design (UK), Sheffield Hallam University (UK), the University of Venice (Italy), and the Technion Institute of Technology (Israel).

While the theme of the conference centered on providing opportunities for collaboration between medicine and design, its main goal was the facilitation of further collaboration between the Vignelli Center for Design Studies and other institutions worldwide with a common commitment to medical design, emphasizing the benefits of inclusive design to the medical community, and advocating for design excellence.

In a large academic institution like RIT, where thousands of well-educated, driven individuals study and work, projects with similar goals often begin at campus locations with limited or no opportunities for true interdisciplinary collaboration. And although activities focused on the medical and healthcare context had been in progress at RIT before the conference took place, design disciplines often experienced limited collaborative participation with them.

It was this idea of bringing design expertise along with that of technology and science onto the same stage that was the real achievement of the conference and of Roger's vision. This allowed an opportunity to exemplify how design acts as a bridge between rational/analytical thinking and intuitive/humanistic thinking to aid in addressing global issues such as those in medicine, healthcare, and accessibility.

Roger's initiative was successful.
It increased awareness of shared interests and the potential for future collaborations to address crucial human needs by departments and disciplines at RIT and our partners worldwide.

This conference sparked new ideas, opportunities, and ultimately new collaborative projects for our students in the years following the event.
Some such initiatives included:

• Industrial design and engineering projects via multidisciplinary design programs at the Kate Gleason College of Engineering;

• IdeaLab, a Simone Center for Innovation and Entrepreneurship program designed to link unique problems and challenges with creative and technical problem solvers at RIT;

• Studio930 summer program, a design consultancy offering collaborative and interdisciplinary opportunities for students to work on accessibility and medical care challenges;

• User-centered design and technology, accessibility and inclusion for individuals of all abilities;

• Studio projects designed for underserved communities around the world.

These programs included collaboration and expert support from
Rochester Regional Health (RRH) and
Al Sigl Community of Agencies.

Roger's vision, championed in 2014, has provided a global platform at RIT from which inclusive design solutions and design thinking methodologies in the medical and healthcare fields are emphasized. More importantly, however, through his leadership, he exemplified the highest moral and educational values on behalf of all participants and particularly on behalf of the design disciplines represented.

Thank you, Roger, for your vision, leadership, and perseverance.

Student work from Dan Harel's industrial design courses, 2011–2016 Image compilation by Dan Harel

2011 - 2016

Connections
Over Six Decades

Doug Wadden
Designer, Educator
Professor Emeritus
University of Washington
Seattle

Education is what remains after one has forgotten what one has learned in school.
ALBERT EINSTEIN

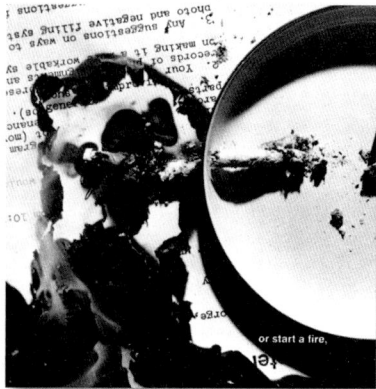

I have known Roger Remington since 1965. I was a student at RIT, majoring in photography and also taking courses in design while interning in the Corporate Communications Department at Xerox, and Roger was a young instructor at the school. I transitioned to graphic design in graduate school and eventually relocated to Seattle in 1970 to teach at the University of Washington. Roger and I have visited numerous times over the years, participating in design conferences, international congresses, and academic meetings.

We share a common interest in the roots of American modernism and the movements associated with it. For Roger, this has been the focus of much of his scholarship and his efforts to create a significant design legacy in the collections that now constitute the Vignelli Center for Design Studies. For myself, it grew out of my RIT education in modernist photography and merged easily with my design education at Yale. Roger has devoted himself to advancing design by embracing history and documenting work that contributes to the education of academic and professional design communities nationally and internationally. We both want design to possess clarity, authenticity, and to contribute to society.

For each of us, teaching has been a pathway to scholarship. For Roger, that has resulted in original research and significant publications. For me, it has been teaching at a major public research university with design practice as creative scholarship.

We both owe a great deal to RIT, and to our design students and colleagues over the last six decades. We are inspired by many friends and associates in our respective communities, by peers in the numerous AIGA chapters, and by fellow members in the Alliance Graphique Internationale. I have tried to capture much of this in my monograph *Practice What You Teach* and include these images from our shared Rochester past and my parallel career in Seattle. Roger has established an enviable record of achievement and longevity that will be difficult to surpass, and that RIT will surely miss.

Left:
Xerox, corporate brochure, 1966, from a series of photographic illustrations
All images: design by Douglas Wadden

Above:
Untitled, 1967, photo-serigraph from my senior thesis based on figure studies

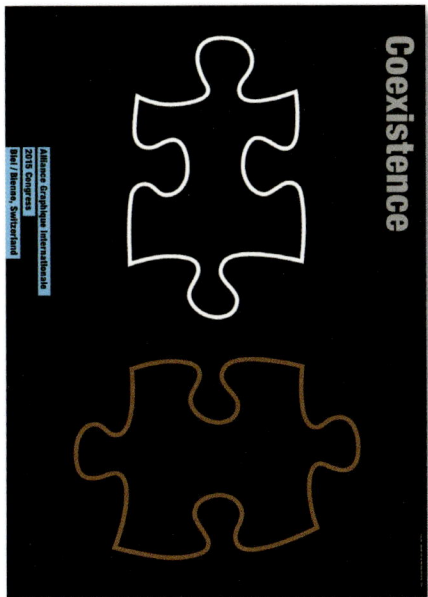

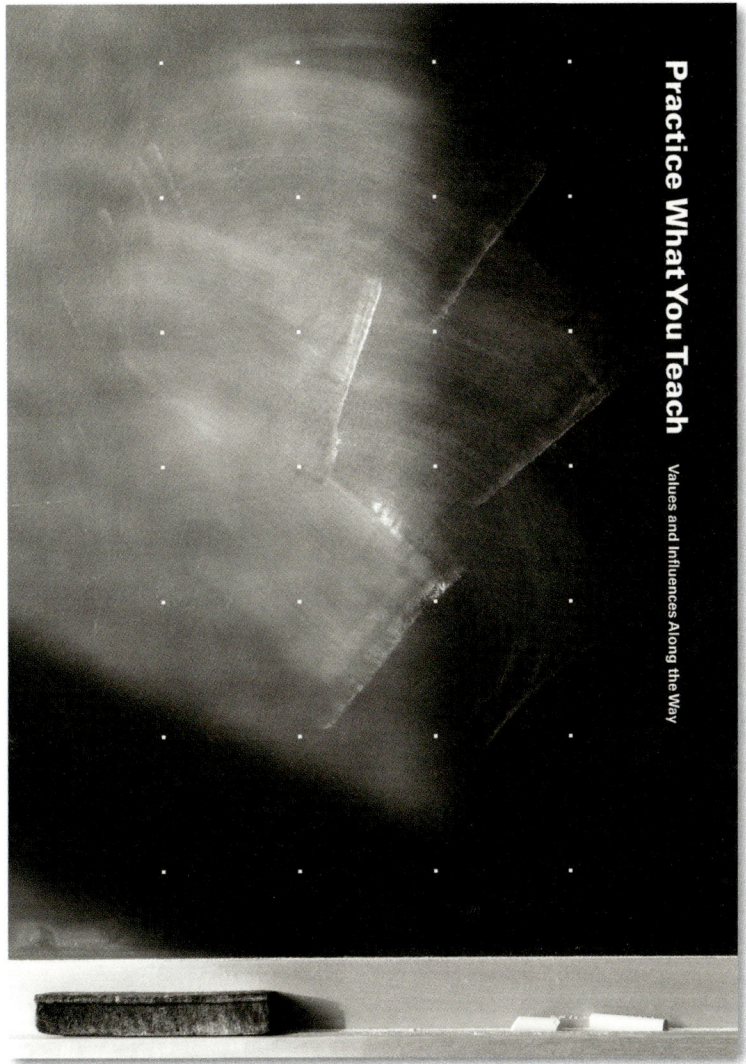

Left, above:
Coexistence, congress poster, 2015,
Alliance Graphique Internationale,
Bienne, Switzerland

Left, below:
Universal/Unique, 1988, International
Invitational Exhibition,
University of the Arts, Philadelphia

Right, above:
Practice What You Teach:
Values and Influences Along
the Way, 2015,
Self-published monograph of
my work spanning fifty years

An Extraordinary Contribution to Education

Félix Beltrán
Doctor Honoris Causa
Educator
Distinguished Professor
Universidad Autónoma Metropolitana
Mexico City

Opposite:
Homage to R. Roger Remington
Design by Félix Beltrán, 2020
Photo by Elizabeth Lamark

More than 40 years have passed since I discovered R. Roger Remington. Despite the time that has passed, I remember it was a 1974 logo for a Rochester automotive parts manufacturer that first piqued my curiosity about his design work. Later it was Roger's books. From *Nine Pioneers in American Graphic Design* to his most recent, *Logo Modernism*, Roger has contributed significantly to our understanding of the history of modern design.

I also wish to emphasize Roger's contribution to design education, which I have had knowledge of through conversations with Massimo and Lella Vignelli, as well as Hermann Zapf, among others. Roger clearly understood and conveyed both the practical and social aspects of graphic design.

It is easy to say that Roger taught for fifty-seven years. It is difficult, however, to assess in a few lines his impact in its broadest and most complete sense. An education that is only dazzled by technological advances does not emphasize that education has two aspects: the development of design abilities and the directing of those abilities toward society.

These words will never be enough of a tribute to R. Roger Remington's contribution to culture, and not just in the United States.

Vignelli: Photographs

Gary Hustwit
Filmmaker and Photographer

Massimo Vignelli had a huge impact on my life and career. In 2005, he was the first designer I approached to be in my first film, *Helvetica*, and he was also the first on-camera interview I ever conducted. In a way, he helped launch my career as a filmmaker. I'm lucky that I was able to spend a lot of time with him and his wife, Lella, who was his partner in life and design. Together they had a career that spanned over fifty years and almost as many disciplines: graphic design, product design, corporate identity, wayfinding, installations, architecture, furniture, jewelry, clothing, and so much more.

In May of 2013, I was getting more interested in still photography and, frankly, I just wanted willing subjects I could photograph in order to get better at it. I thought about interesting people I knew in New York who might let me spend the day with them and be photographed, so I emailed Massimo and he graciously agreed.

I arrived at the Vignellis' apartment on the Upper East Side, where they'd lived for over thirty years. My main goal was to try to capture what it felt like being in that space with them at that point in their lives. Massimo always said a designer should be able to design everything "from a spoon to a city," so nearly everything in the house was designed by them... the furniture, lighting, vases, dishes, cutlery. I spent hours photographing the contents of their bookshelves, their kitchen, everything.

I'm not sure why I'm obsessed with the little details in people's homes and studios. The contents of a cupboard, or the variety of books and mementos sitting on a shelf. I think examining those details is just an easy way to glean more information about someone, what they love, why they do what they do. I find that I spend a lot of time in my films focusing on those details.

I took over four hundred photographs that day, and didn't really have plans to do anything with them. But as the years passed, I saw these images as a kind of time capsule, a document of a day in the life of two incredible people I admired, who were no longer with us. Looking at these images now, I'm struck by the range and brilliance of their design careers, and by their undying love for each other. Luckily, a conversation with Roger led to the publication of a book of these photos and a wonderful exhibition at the Vignelli Center.

Sometimes a camera can capture a moment, or a sense of place, but it's impossible to sum up two lives with a handful of images taken in one day. I'm grateful that the Vignellis invited me into their home to make these photographs, and I hope that their work, influence, and memory will continue to live on.

Designed to be ›› at the Center

Gene DePrez
Designer, Management Consultant
RIT Graduate (BFA '62, MFA '68)
RIT Colleague, Friend

Though Roger and I did not know each other as design students on the downtown Rochester campus (he had just graduated when I came in as a freshman), we were influenced and shaped by some of the same RIT thought leaders. Among them were Stan Witmeyer, then director of the School of Art and Design, and Hans Barschel, legendary design professor and mentor to both of us in our junior and senior years. A few years after graduation, we were first introduced to each other and began sharing concepts and understandings through the intellectual curiosity of Maurice Kessman, director of educational research, as we collaborated in publishing the interdisciplinary journal *Matrix*. Later, with Roger a leader on the design faculty and my return to RIT as director of communications, we again came together, this time energized by the visionary leadership of President Paul Miller.

Continuing in the spirit of these early mentors, Roger and I became close faculty/staff teammates, occasional business partners, and lifetime friends. In the 1970s, we worked closely with many other university and community leaders to provide opportunities for young student designers to help identify and solve community development and citizen education needs through the Urbanarium—a regional consortium linking students and faculty from across RIT and from other area colleges, working together with institutions, nonprofits, and leaders from government, business, and civic and neighborhood associations. Roger was at the center of this as the program's academic leader, earning RIT national and global recognition as a model of university-community collaboration. The legacy of many of those projects is evidenced today, especially in the renaissance of downtown Rochester, its neighborhoods, and surrounding towns.

Simultaneously, we worked together to design and execute a comprehensive university-wide identity system and graphic mark to strengthen and unify RIT's brand across all the colleges and program areas, communications, publications, correspondence, and signage, much of it adapted and still in use today, four decades later.

R. Roger Remington early in his career at RIT
Photo by Professor Robert Keough

Above all, Roger's most important legacy is his envisioning and bringing to life the Vignelli Center for Design Studies. This unique global resource would not have been realized without Roger's diligence, vision, and persuasive powers. I saw this firsthand. At the request of Roger and his dean at the time, I chaired the School of Design's National Business Advisory Committee which, after meeting with Massimo and Lella Vignelli, quickly rallied around advancing the idea of the Vignelli Center. Meeting frequently at their studio and residence in New York and in Rochester, we were able to help focus the idea and gain the support Roger needed to advance the themes of education, advocacy, preservation, collaboration, the public good, and globalism. These are the same values I have associated with Roger from my first years of knowing him, so long ago. His work honors not only his efforts but also those mentors and thought leaders who influenced us in those earliest years.

Fortune *magazine cover illustration, undated*
Design by Hans J. Barschel
Cary Graphic Design Archive
Gift of R. Roger Remington

To Capture the Essence of a Message in an Image

Inge Druckrey
Professor Emerita
University of the Arts
Philadelphia

Opposite, left:
Beethoven
Poster for the Yale
Symphony Orchestra
1979, offset lithograph
Design by Inge Druckrey

Opposite, right:
Poster for the Yale Women's Forum
ca. 1975, offset lithograph
Design by Inge Druckrey,
Photography by Keri Keating

To Roger Remington

I might have met you for the first time in the mid-1960s, through Rob Roy Kelly, when I taught with Rob at the Kansas City Art Institute, or at one of the Aspen Design Conferences. It seems to me that I have known you for a long time.

In the mid-1980s, I vividly remember some event at RIT, when the computer was still very new, at least for me, when you showed us experiments with a new computer software—I think it was Hypertext—that might be applicable to the study of the history of graphic design. (This is a very vague recollection.) It was also the time when you published your first book on the history of graphic design in the United States. Several others followed soon after. All of that should have, but did not, give me a hint of what your focus and contribution to graphic design would be.

I met you, through the years, at many conferences, lectures, and design events, where you and Bruce Meader were always present, quietly observing.

Around 2017, you invited Hans Allemann and me to give a talk on our work, as well as a recorded interview. All this seemed in no way out of the ordinary, but for you all this fit into a larger plan.

I was close to eighty years old, and Hans was about to leave the US and settle back in Switzerland. For you, we were both mosaic pieces within the larger picture of the history of graphic design in the United States in the twentieth and beginning twenty-first century; therefore you made sure to have a record. You also asked both of us to send samples of our work for the archive. All this happened quietly, nearly "by the way," and that is typical for you. You remind me of Adrian Frutiger and Hans Eduard Meier, who both had made major contributions to type design of the twentieth century but had retained this quiet simplicity.

Your contribution to graphic design is huge. The creation of the Vignelli Center for Design Studies at RIT and, most importantly, setting up a professional archive for graphic design in the United States, are a major step to give graphic design the same cultural importance as architecture and the fine arts. Many of us thought about setting up archives, at least at the art schools where we taught, but no one I know did it.

Thank you, Roger.

Friday October 12 1979 8:00 pm Woolsey Hall Admission free
Yale Symphony Orchestra

Beethoven Robert Kapilow Music Director
Piano Concerto no.5 "Emperor" C Geanakoplos Soloist
Symphony no.5

H O V E N

Yale
celebrates
women's
achievements
in today's
world

Preservation: A High Calling

Jared Stahler
Senior Pastor, Saint Peter's Church
New York City

When, in 1974, Lella and Massimo Vignelli interviewed to contract for the graphic design of the "new Saint Peter's Church" at Citicorp Center, no one—certainly not the Vignellis—knew the scope of the project would soon expand so dramatically. Nor would anyone perceive how important the project would become in their vast output. A series of turns with architect, client, and the wider community would lead an initial contract for graphics to become a contract whereby the Vignellis designed everything: interiors, liturgical objects, furniture, vestments. Massimo would even argue for, and succeed in making, architectural changes in coordination with Hugh Stubbins and W. Easley Hamner of Stubbins Associates, as well as completely overhauling the facade and console design of the organ being built in Bonn, Germany, by Klais Orgelbau.

Later in life, Massimo was fond of telling the story his own way: "When I received the call asking me if I would design the new Saint Peter's, I thought it was Saint Peter's, Rome. 'Yes, Holy Father, I'll take the job. The logo is great, but the rest has to go.'"

For two designers who functioned at their very best as one—for this one design team to delve into one design function after another—the "new Saint Peter's Church" at 54th Street and Lexington Avenue in New York City was both a challenge and an opportunity of a lifetime. They consistently spoke of it as "our most important project." Indeed, it is the fullest embodiment of their highest guiding principle: design is one.

Perhaps it is both their intense collaboration on the project and the comprehensive nature of the project that make Saint Peter's Church so important to their legacy. Yes, and likely it is at least two additional elements.

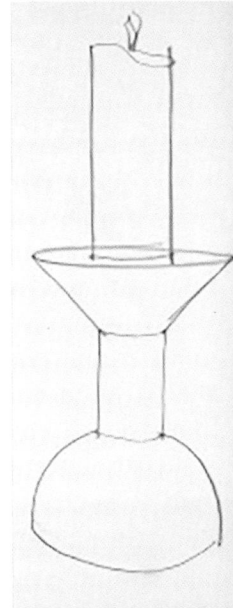

Two elements where you, Roger, and I come into the story.

First, Saint Peter's is a Vignelli design that will endure. In part it will endure owing to the notion that conservation is foundational to the church. As an institution, the church has never really been in the fast lane of change. As a community of people looking to the future, the church interacts with the present by reflecting on the past. To be sure, there are both downsides and upsides to being a conservator of things cultural, theological, sociological, historical. As for the preservation of a gem of late modernism, certainly this characteristic of the church is a benefit.

Opposite:
Saint Peter's Church oak candlestick sketch
(pencil on paper) by Massimo Vignelli
Photo of candlestick by George Cserna
From the Massimo and Lella Vignelli papers

Left:
Saint Peter's Church postcards of
liturgical items
Designed by Massimo and Lella Vignelli
Photography by George Cserna
From the Massimo and Lella Vignelli papers

Below:
Saint Peter's Church postcard
Photo by George Cserna
From the Massimo and Lella Vignelli papers

But conservation does not happen on its own. Your leadership of the Vignelli Center, your work as a scholar of design, and your passion for the Saint Peter's project in particular, all contribute mightily to the preservation of this place, its objects, its graphic design, and its vision for "life in the City." Today we are New York City's youngest landmark and we are on our way to being designated a state and national historic landmark. Good design calls us to attend to its preservation. While you may be retiring from RIT, I am thankful you will remain engaged in preserving what we both hold so near to our hearts.

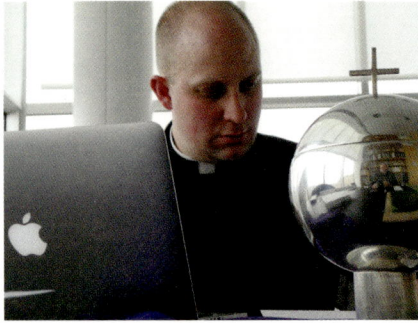

Second, Saint Peter's is a Vignelli design that is, above all else, about people. People have always been the driving force for Lella and Massimo. I came to know this truth in their home. Like you, I have sat at every table in their home. Massimo's steel desk. Lella's desk with Pomodoro legs. The marble dining table. The kitchen table. Massimo was thrilled the day I acquired a Metafora table. These tables have long fostered conversation, finished design and discarded design, formal and informal meals, the all-important afternoon espresso. Many are the memories. Many are the friendships forged.

Above:
Jared Stahler
in R. Roger Remington's office
Vignelli Center for Design Studies
Photo by R. Roger Remington

Right:
Saint Peter's Church,
God's table and pews
Designed by Lella and Massimo Vignelli
Photo by Bruce Ian Meader

No wonder that at Saint Peter's the altar is so integral to the space. Its wood slats extending to just about every surface, making the entire church seem almost one great big table. "God's table," Lella's determined and constant refrain reminds us.

As a historian of design, you can trace the formal elements of these objects. As a pastor, I ponder the continuous flow of people brought together by God's table, every table. As I write this, I think of the table at the French restaurant on Second Avenue that you and I like so much, and your and Suzanne's table when you hosted me in your home. And, I am thinking of that great table—likely redesigned by Lella and Massimo—of the heavenly banquet, the foretaste of which has become a sustaining force in your life. Ultimately, what we find at each of these tables is a gift: the human spirit at its best. Wonderful, marvelous, creative, kind, loving, dedicated. People.

In short, Roger, what we are called to preserve is not simply good design itself, but the good design does for others. Looking back at your long and distinguished career, you—and the designers you have both taught and studied—have championed precisely this. Yours is a high calling well fulfilled.

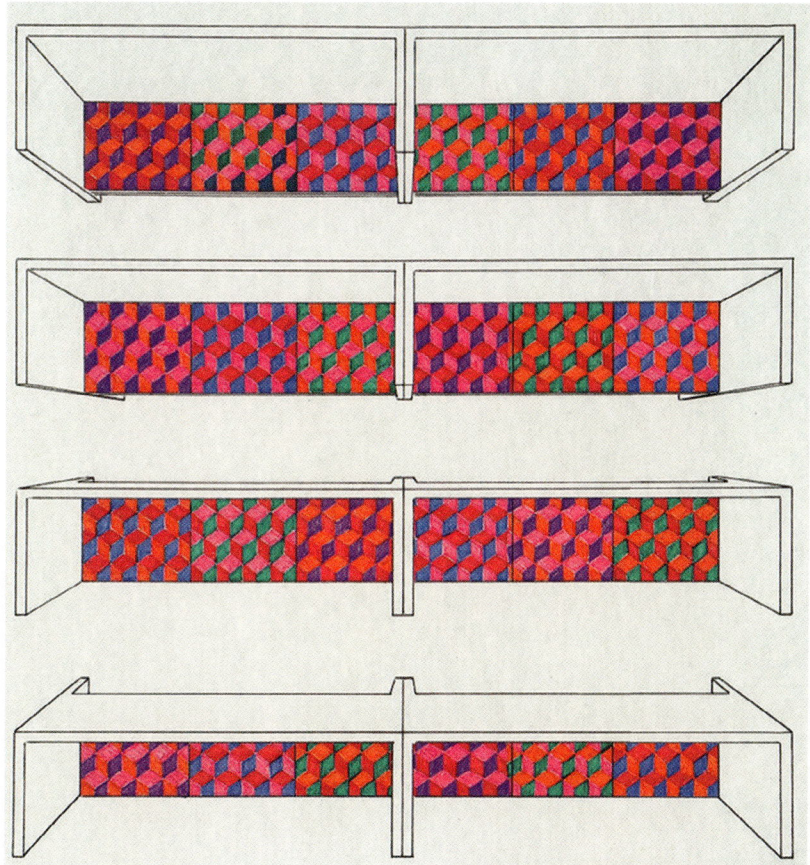

Above:
Sketches for Saint Peter's Church
Pew cushions
Ink on board
Designed by Lella Vignelli
From the Massimo and Lella Vignelli papers

Right:
Detail of needlepoint cushions for
Saint Peter's Church pew
Designed by Lella Vignelli
From the Massimo and Lella Vignelli papers

Saving the Past,
Inspiring the Future

Jennifer Whitlock
Archivist
Vignelli Center for Design Studies
Rochester Institute of Technology
Rochester, NY

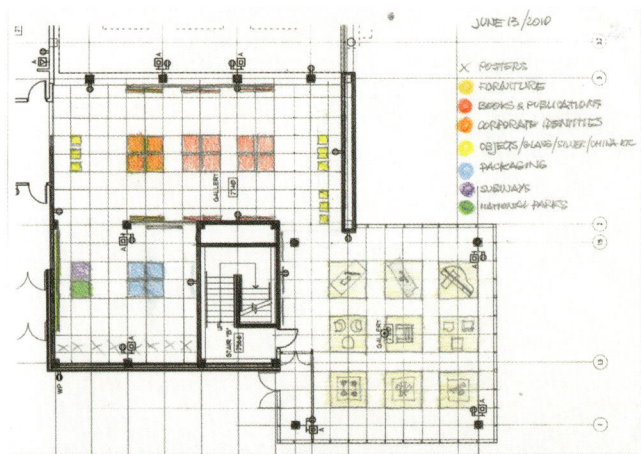

From the archives of
Vignelli Associates
475 Tenth Avenue
New York, NY 10018
212 244 1919 Ext. 15

Please return materials!

Department of Communication Design
College of Fine and Applied Arts
Rochester Institute of Technology

December 21, 1972

Mr. Massimo Vignelli
Unimark International
410 East 62nd Street
New York, New York

Dear Mr. Vignelli:

I have read with much interest of your development of the
"International Grid System" for Knoll.

If possible could you send me materials which describe this
plan in detail. We are in the process of building a visual
design resource library for our students and I feel that
material such as your Knoll Grid System is important.

Sincerely,

R. Roger Remington
Chairman

One Lomb Memorial Drive
Rochester, New York 14623

Opposite, clockwise:
*Layout sketch of the future Vignelli
Center by Massimo Vignelli
From the Massimo and Lella
Vignelli papers*

*Archives vault at the Vignelli Center
for Design Studies
Photo by Jennifer Whitlock*

*Vignelli Associates' archive label
From the Massimo and Lella
Vignelli papers*

*Exterior, Vignelli Center for Design Studies
Photo by Jennifer Whitlock*

*Left:
R. Roger Remington to Massimo Vignelli
re "the Grid," 1972
From the Massimo and Lella
Vignelli papers*

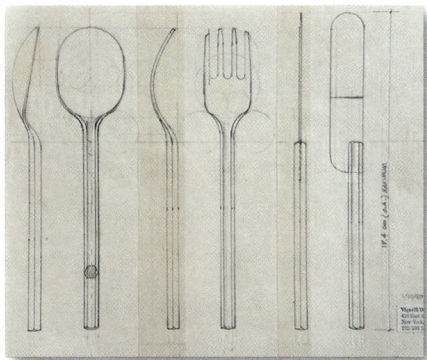

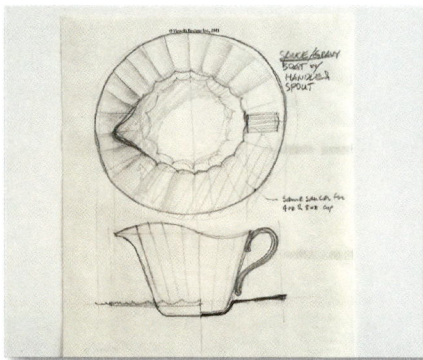

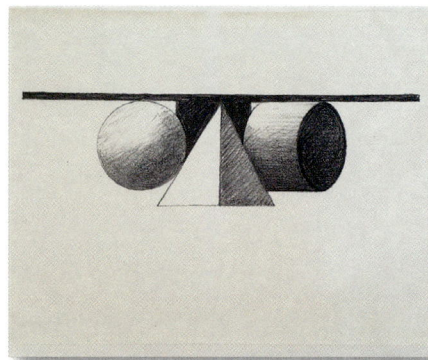

Top, left:
Ciga Hotel silverware drawing
by David B. Law, Senior Vice President,
Vignelli Associates, 1980

Bottom, left:
Ciga Hotel silverware, 1980
Design by Lella and Massimo Vignelli

Top, center:
Calegaro Pavillion drawing
by David B. Law, Senior Vice President,
Vignelli Associates, 1981

Bottom, center:
Calegaro Pavillion gravy boat and saucer
designed by Lella and Massimo Vignelli
and David B. Law, Senior Vice President,
Vignelli Associates

Top right:
Casigliani Metafora No. 1 table
pencil sketch
Table design by Lella and Massimo Vignelli

Bottom right:
Casigliani Metafora No. 1 table
product information brochure
Design by Lella and Massimo Vignelli

*All artifacts these pages from the
Massimo and Lella Vignelli Papers
Vignelli Center for Design Studies
Photos by Jennifer Whitlock*

*Above:
Display in the Vignelli Center for Design
Studies Archives, 2019
Curated by Jennifer Whitlock and RIT
students Carmen Ibis Lopez, Leah Green,
and Samantha Cleveland in 2019*

*Top, right:
Detail of NYCTA Subway Guide, 1972
Designed by Massimo Vignelli and
Joan Charysyn*

*Bottom, right:
American Airlines Annual Report
Sketch by Massimo Vignelli*

Roger Remington
at RIT, 1963–2020

Jeremy Myerson
Helen Hamlyn Professor of Design
Royal College of Art, London

1963

2020

Global fears over missiles	Global fears over microbes
"I Want To Hold Your Hand"	"I Want To Wash My Hands"
Hitchcock's *The Birds*	*Godzilla vs. Kong*
Design for business	Design for all
Gas 29 cents per gallon	Gas 2.3 dollars per gallon
JFK shot in Dallas	Trump tweets
Buick Riviera	Kia Soul Electric Vehicle
Alcatraz closes	Guantanamo Bay stays open
Sylvia Plath's *The Bell Jar*	Hilary Mantel's *The Mirror & the Light*
"I Have a Dream"	"Nobody builds walls better than me"
Barefoot in the Park on Broadway	*Hamilton* on Broadway
Pop art by Roy Lichtenstein	Donald Judd retrospective at MoMA
Cassette tape	Artificial intelligence
Lennon is 23	McCartney is 78

*Best wishes from the
Helen Hamlyn Centre for Design,
Royal College of Art, London*

A Former Student's Viewpoint

Jerry Infantino
Class of 1969, RIT
School of Art and Design

The Bevier building sits at the corner of South Washington and Spring streets, at the heart of the old RIT campus, and it is there where I first met Roger Remington. The beautiful old building, erected in 1910, stood in sharp contrast to the modern ideas of a man whose life would eventually become dedicated to the preservation of international contemporary design and the teachings of leading-edge designers. Internationally recognized and professionally awarded over his long career, he has influenced countless students. It is his forward-thinking ideas that have brought him to this milestone event today.

I am unaware of how many contributors to this book are prior students of Roger's, but I'd like to present a few thoughts from a once-young student's point of view. I remember walking into his classroom in 1966 and being struck by his peaceful demeanor, his gentlemanly presence, and his perfectly clear presentation of the subject matter. There he stood in front of the class, in his sport coat, button-down shirt and tie, looking every bit the part of a college prof. The classrooms in the old Bevier building had huge windows that filled the rooms with natural light. The feeling was one of freedom and discovery. There was no better man to guide a young bunch of art students through the first days of our design education than an energetic young instructor with a deliberate and purposeful style. His manner was patient and measured and, like the man we know today, he practiced the thoughtful and kind prodding of a true educator. One could feel his passion for the work and his respect for the process he so gracefully bestowed.

I will leave the professional side of his vast contribution to others in this book. Instead, I would like to emphasize the attributes of the person I know as a teacher, a neighbor, and a friend.

Roger and I lived across the street from one another and would chat on the sidewalk from time to time. It won't surprise anyone to know he was the same inquisitive and gentle person we found in the classroom. Never in a hurry, he would show an interest in what was going on in the life of one of his students, thirty years later. Maybe it was his interest in the results of his labors, but he made an effort to stay in touch with many of my fellow students from the class of '69. We likewise have invited him as a special guest to our luncheons and reunions.

The Bevier building, Rochester, NY
Photo by Jerry Infantino

The best part of having Roger in our lives today is witnessing how he enjoys the continuation of the story that started long ago in downtown Rochester. A story in which he was, and is, an important part. Without a professor like Roger in our lives, our RIT experience would have been diminished. Rarely will we find a man who has so diligently followed a path forward with a singular focus on design education, a man whose mission in life is so clearly defined by excellence, preservation of an art form, and the development of future designers.

Visiting the Distinguished Professor in his Vignelli Center office, one can sense the happiness and satisfaction of a life well lived. Roger's work has culminated in an expression of his personal vision and stands today, as it will for years to come. His influence will continue to touch those who pass through RIT and the design center he helped to build. On behalf of the students who were the beneficiaries of his thoughtfulness, his foresight, and his leadership, we say thank you, Mister Remington. Good going, Rog.

Jerry Infantino
Class of 1969, RIT
School of Art and Design

Reflections of a Remarkable Career

Jill Wagner, MFA
Educator, Designer
RIT Graduate

Humbly he will tell you, "I had a little something to do with that." In his fifty-seven years as an educator and designer, R. Roger Remington helped create a nationally recognized design program at RIT.

He was internationally recognized for erecting a monument that will continue to shape design education. The Vignelli Center for Design Studies, an institution dedicated to the future of design and to preserving its history, is a vital focal point for scholars, friends, and students interested in design. Thanks to Roger's steadfast ability to acquire archives and to orchestrate and host traveling exhibits, guest speakers, demonstrations, and other exciting events, the center has strengthened the academic profile of RIT.

In the course of his academic career, Roger acquired design collections of modernist American graphic design pioneers such as Lester Beall, Will Burtin, Cipe Pineles, William Golden, and Alvin Lustig, among others. He hosted lecture series and symposiums by preeminent designers and educators, published seven books on design history, produced exhibits and documentaries, and launched international exchange programs with the Anhalt University of Applied Sciences in Dessau, Germany, a program in Copenhagen, Denmark, and a graduate program in Design Studies.

Roger is the longest serving faculty member at RIT and, before his retirement, held the Vignelli Distinguished Professorship. His students and colleagues have added to his legacy and have entered academic institutions as professors, published books, and maintained successful design businesses. Many students have fond memories of their interactions with Roger, who went out of his way to include students in exclusive projects and meetings. Roger not only gave his students access to most of his academic resources but was a friend and confidant during times of need.

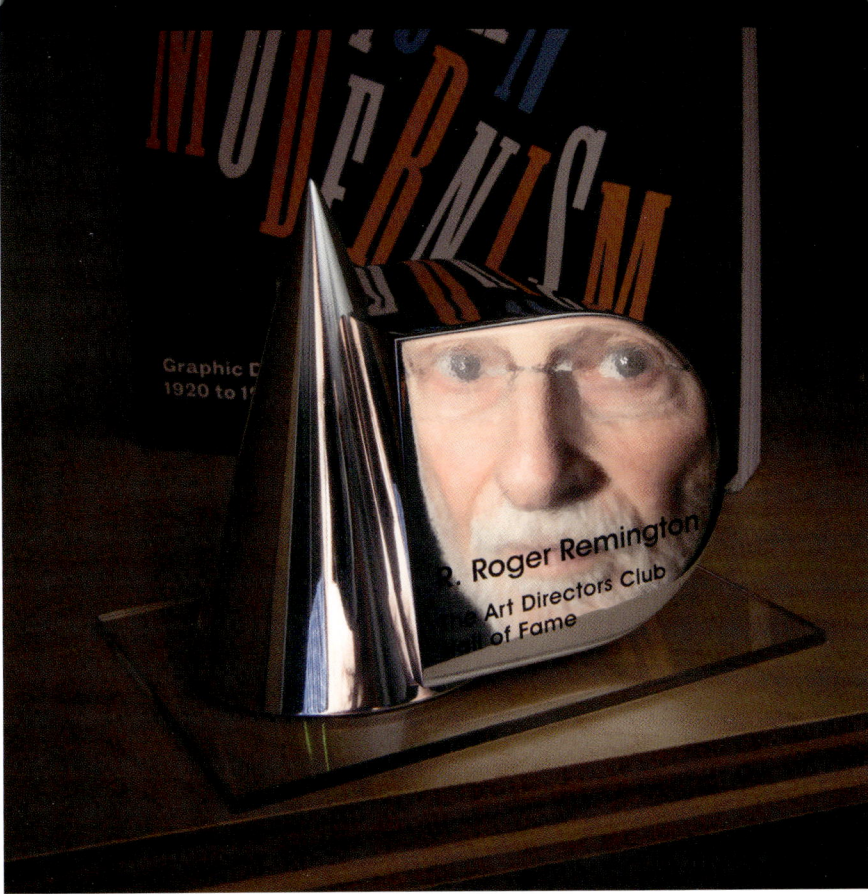

R. Roger Remington with award
Photo 8 x 8 inches, 2020
Design by Jill Wagner
Photo by John Retallack

Over the years, Roger has earned many accolades that recognize his enormous contribution to the education and preservation of graphic design history. The golden groundbreaking shovels and awards bestowed upon him are a crowning achievement, a reflection of his long career. It must have been hard to mark the end of a fifty-seven-year tenure with a retirement announcement, especially looking back at his accomplishments. The faculty and students of RIT felt like family, and to some he will always be connected through a special bond. His legacy lies not only in the archives he acquired and preserved, the buildings he erected, and the pages of books and articles he published—it's coupled with the pages, products, and pedagogy that are passed on from his students to a new generation of designers.

Go forth...
do good design!

Joe A. Watson
RIT Colleague
MFA, Yale, 1961

This page:
Collage from left to right:
"hand-rendered comps"
"control central early on"
"early spring at RIT"
"Merry Christmas, Ruth"
"the dream realized"
"Great connections"
"one-on-one everyone"
"110 seniors that year"
"1975 B.C."
Design and photography by Joe Watson

Opposite:
Image of Roger pointing
"go forth... do good design!"
Design and Photography by Joe Watson

Roger Remington and Joe Watson
Photo by Joan Hantz

go forth... do good design!

Roger, you have been my friend and colleague for over forty-five years. I have enjoyed watching you do the political dance, delicately and precisely, through the local, national, and international academic maze to accomplish, over time, a truly great leap forward for modernism in design—but really, more importantly, simply to sustain the pursuit of excellence in design in all its permutations.

Over fifty years in the effort, you are truly the consummate long-distance runner. To do this, of course, you started with an insatiable love for and interest in design. You became a great teacher. Your approach has been wide reaching but, at the same time, focused as to an individual student's direction... and, of course, all in terms of design at the highest level.

You helped move the field from commercial art to graphic design. This shift was made clear in the numerous scholarly books you have authored, along with the biographies of the outstanding designers in the field.

As professor, designer, scholar, author, artist, historian, facilitator, and visionary, you have presented the "how to do it," the "why to do it," and, with the biographies, the "who did it best." But best of all, like all great teachers, you made your students love to do it.

You leave RIT after the culmination of your career-long goal of establishing a comprehensive design archive. In addition to securing for the archive the work of many of the world's finest designers, you, along with the Vignellis, also secured the funds to build the building to house the collection and to continue the life of this unique study facility. Nice job, Roger! What took you so long?

Running alongside all these monumental accomplishments, there have been many outbursts of your explosive laughter, the laughter that does not build but comes out at full volume from the very start. So it's always fun to give you a good one-liner and just stand back!

With love and appreciation,
Joe A. Watson
RIT Professor Emeritus
and your program's
First Token Yalie

John T. Hill
Designer, Author, Photographer, Educator
Cofounder and First Chair
Department of Photography
Yale School of Art
Executor, Walker Evans Estate

Human Society, the world,
and the whole of mankind is
to be found in the alphabet.
VICTOR HUGO

For years, scientists have been collecting animal and plant specimens as a primary source. R. Roger Remington has been making a similar repository of graphic design for over thirty years. It is thorough and unique and will inspire generations to come.

The intelligence, passion, focus, and stamina devoted to this tireless pursuit of so many years represent the singularity that is Roger.

These treasures go beyond being a rich collection of design studies, to preserve clues to our cultural history. Yale University Professor of Graphic Design Walker Evans strongly believed that our deepest and most telling sensibilities are found in the rendering of the alphabet. This includes vernacular advertising, signs, and most printed matter. The fonts, materials, strokes, words, and the patina, tell us who we were.

The sign to the right is a prime example of Evans's art of appropriation. Among its many layers are two simple words expressing our thoughts for a dear friend.

Roger, we thank you for the trove that you leave us.

RRR
JEK

John Koegel
RIT MFA Graduate, RIT Faculty
and Colleague

John Koegel
RIT MFA Graduate, RIT Faculty
and Colleague

RRR

I first met you as an undergraduate in the Graphic Design program at RIT. One day in your *Women Pioneers in Graphic Design* course, you brought in your Hasselblad camera. In that moment, I knew you were going to be OK.

When Massimo and Lella Vignelli began to bring their lifetime-of-design collection to RIT, you encouraged me to assist the Vignellis to set up the Benetton Gallery. Massimo would often take the time to discuss his work with me. The opportunity to work with the Vignellis was the ultimate dream come true. I skipped all my classes for weeks while helping them in the gallery!

After obtaining my BFA, I entered the Computer Graphic Design graduate program at RIT. My connection to the Vignelli Center continued to grow stronger. I remained your student and became your graduate assistant while delving into graphic and computer graphic design.

While still working on my MFA in computer graphic design, I began to work full-time in administration for the College of Imaging Arts and Sciences.

After we had several conversations, you finally encouraged (prodded) me to teach at the university. My first course was in computer design, while your hope was that I would teach courses directly related to the Vignelli Center and the Cary Graphic Design Archives.

In the fall of 2020, I began teaching Design Praxis II, a course that engaged graduate design students to create work that activated the archives through new and relevant technologies such as augmented reality.

Because of you, I have remained associated with the Vignelli Center for Design Studies throughout my entire undergraduate and graduate years and beyond, for the past eleven years and counting.

RRR, you have been my teacher, mentor, colleague, and dear friend. It is an honor and privilege to know you and to share amazing intellectual conversations and a bit of that Remington humor.

Never forget the road trip!
JEK

Above:
Will Burtin's The Communication of Knowledge *exhibition, 1971*
Photo by Carol Burtin Fripp

Right, all images:
The Communication of Knowledge, *2018*
augmented reality exhibit, various views
Photos by John Koegel
with Microsoft HoloLens

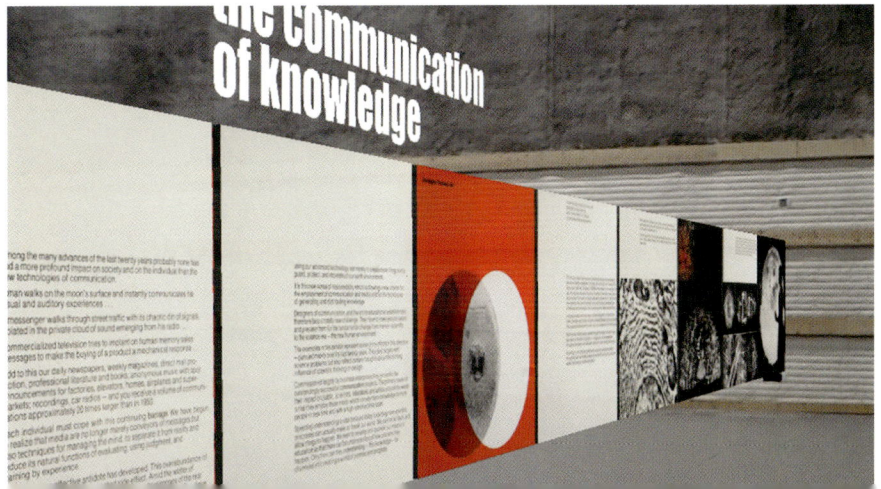

For Roger,
**Designer and Teacher of
Sublime Systems**

John Malinoski
Designer, Educator, RIT Graduate

This page:
Leadership, 2020
gouache, Plaka, and ink
Design by John Malinoski

Opposite:
Growth, 2020
gouache, Plaka, and ink
Design by John Malinoski

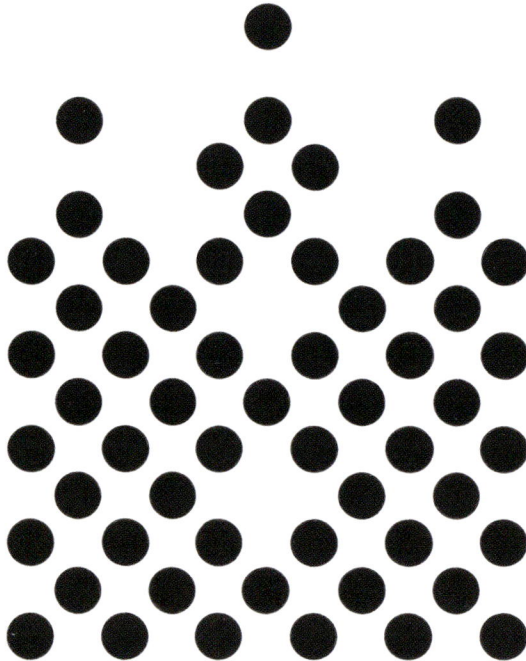

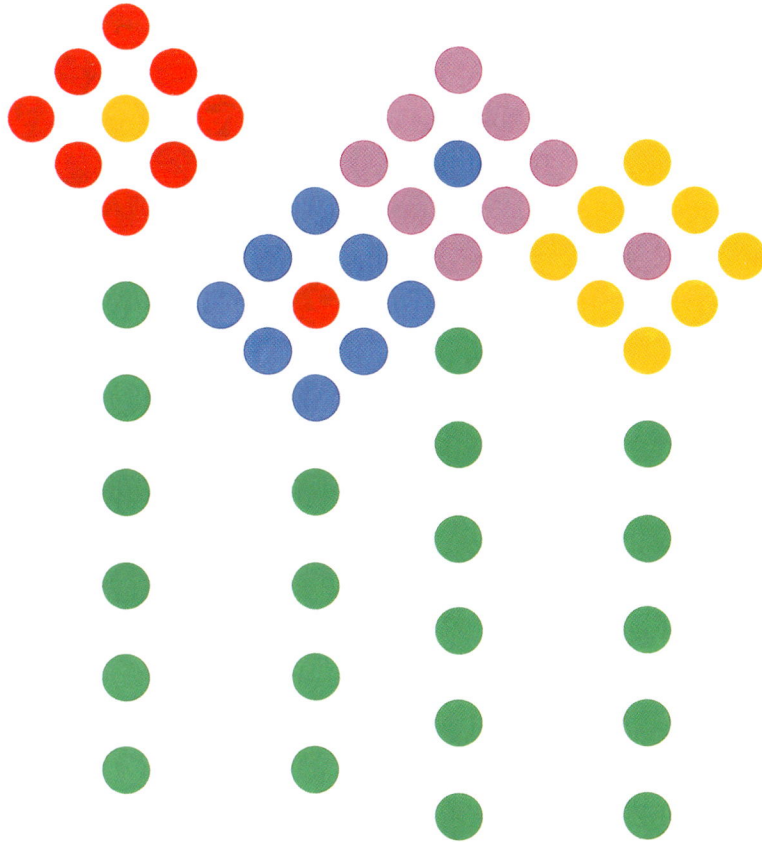

Josh Owen
Vignelli Distinguished Professor of Design
Director, Vignelli Center for
Design Studies, RIT

Honoring Legacy

In honor of Roger Remington's retirement, I had the good fortune to be asked to craft a medal, meant to commemorate the Vignelli Distinguished Professorship, for Roger to wear at his final commencement ceremony at RIT. While this activity required many hands to bring to fruition, the gesture was clear to me from the outset: the object must embody the ethos espoused by the Vignelli Center for Design Studies.

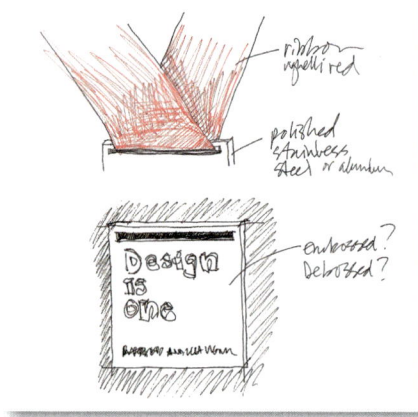

Through its design, this object must serve to identify the wearer as one who preserves the notion of design as a lens through which the problems of the world can be focused and addressed. "Design is one," the philosophy of Massimo and Lella Vignelli, declares that design is a holistic practice, not limited to the categorization often associated with elements of related professions. Wearing the medal carries the responsibility that its host act as a galvanizing force for these related practices—most importantly to use design to advance the common good. Besides conforming to the usability standards associated with any such wearable, this medal would also need to speak clearly and elegantly as signage to those who observe it casually, declaring that it is, in itself, a beacon evocative of the values it asserts.

Mentorship and philosophical lineage are important to me, as they are to any serious designer/educator. One cannot build anew without building upon the existing lessons that humanity has demonstrated collectively. A true steward of lineage is one who synthesizes historical lessons while being an active participant in the ecosystem that extends theory and practice. The Vignelli Distinguished Professor must be this rare polymath, both safeguarding and activating valuable assets from the history of the profession while simultaneously advancing it. This medal holds the symbolic meaning that its bearer delivers on the message branded upon them with it. "Design is one" pronounces its wearer capable of seeing beyond classification, preserving the wisdom of the past while leveraging it to build a better future.

Opposite:
Vignelli Distinguished Professor Medal, 2020
Design by Josh Owen
Photo by Elizabeth Lamark

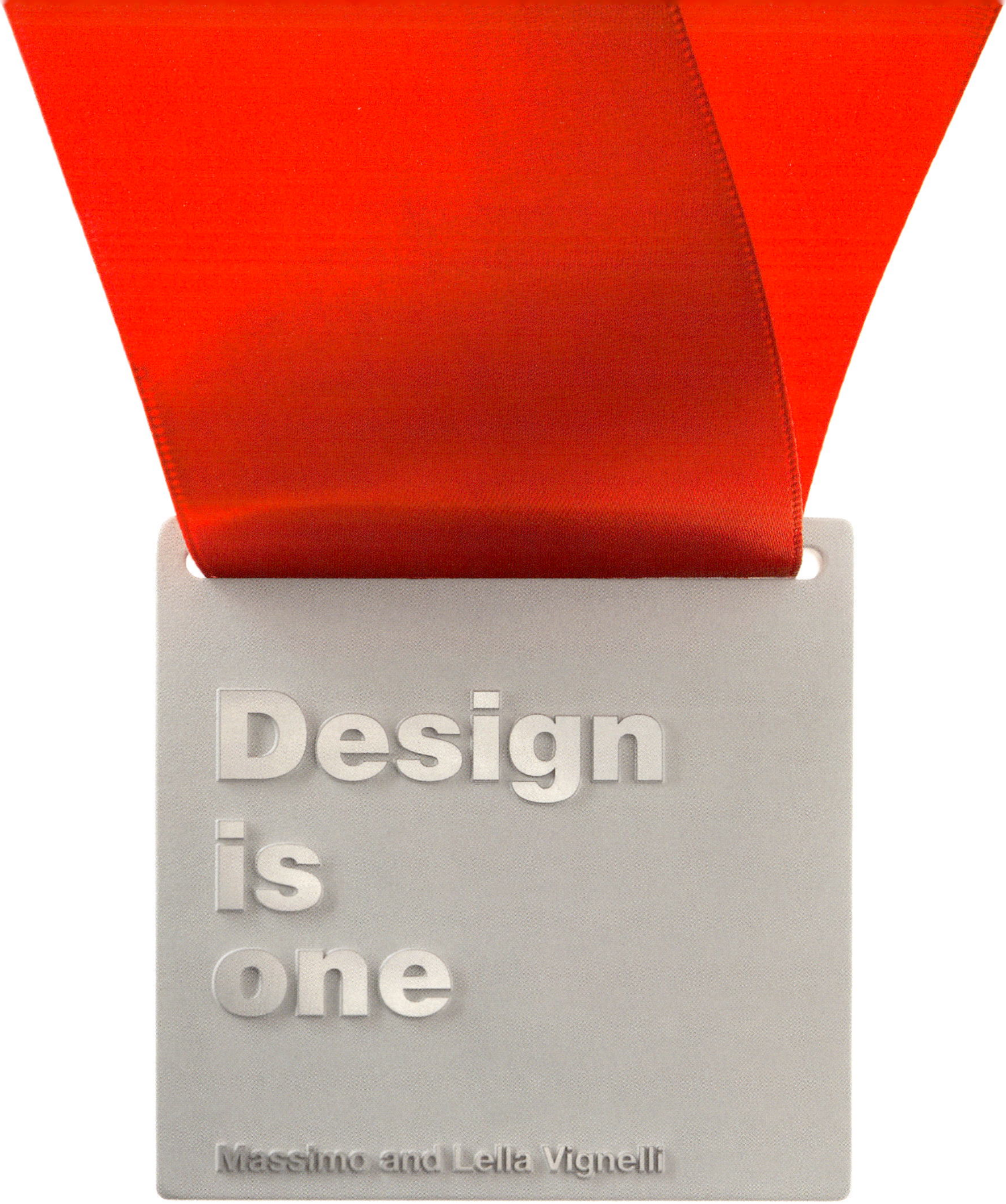
Design
is
one
Massimo and Lella Vignelli

Joyce Hertzson
Educator, Designer, RIT Colleague
Professor, and Program Associate
Vignelli Center for Design Studies

The Long and Crooked Path to Design Studies

This image is an accurate reflection of all of the meetings it has taken to develop Design Studies since its inception in 2010 until now. The changes in description of the program reflect the many iterations the title went through as we tried to find the right path.

MDESIGN STUDIES
Master of Design Studies

MSDESIGN STUDIES
Master of Science in Design Studies

MFADESIGN STUDIES
Master of Fine Arts in Design Studies

VCDDESIGN STUDIES
*Visual Communication Design
Design Studies, etc.*

2010 august 03 MSDESIGN STUDIES september 08 Roger in VC DE

05 MDESIGN STUDIES 10 open VC 11 MDESIGN STUDIES 12 MDESIGN STU

IES 27 DESIGN STUDIES february 03 DESIGN STUDIES 24 DESIGN STUDIE

21 DESIGN STUDIES 28 DESIGN STUDIES may 05 DESIGN STUDIES 12 DI

ber 08 MSDESIGN STUDIES 15 MSDESIGN STUDIES 29 MSDESIGN STUDIE

IES 10 MSDESIGN STUDIES 28 MS/MFA DESIGN STUDIES 30 VC staff dec

STUDIES 11 VC Staff 18 VC Staff 19 MFADESIGN STUDIES 25 VC Staff 26 M

MFA DESIGN STUDIES 22 VC Staff 23 MFA DESIGN STUDIES march 15 VC

STUDIES 19 VC planning 19 MDESIGN STUDIES 26 VC planning 26 MDESIG

12 VC Staff 13 MDESIGN STUDIES 19VC Staff 20 MDESIGN STUDIES 26 VC

18 MDESIGN STUDIES 24 VC staff 25 MDESIGN STUDIES 31 VC Staff nov

january 16 VC Staff 23 VC Staff 30 VC Staff february 06 VC Staff 13 VC S

VC Staff 08 VC Staff 15 MDESIGN STUDIES july 16 DESIGN STUDIES 31 D

Staff october 02 VC Staff 09 MDESIGN STUDIES 16 VC Staff 23 VC Staff 3

january 15 VC Staff 22 VC Staff 29 VC Staff 29 VCDMDESIGN STUDIES f

VC Staff 26 VCDMDESIGN STUDIES march 05 VCDMDESIGN STUDIES

MDESIGN STUDIES 09 VC Staff 09 VCDMDESIGN STUDIES 23 VC Staff 23

14 VCDMDESIGN STUDIES june 25 VC Staff august 06 MS DESIGN ST

Staff november 06 VC Staff 13 VC Staff 20 VC Staff 27 VC Staff decemb

Staff 11 VC Staff 18 VC Staff april 01 VC Staff 08 VC Staff 15 VC Staff 22 VC

ber 09 VC Staff 15 VC Staff 23 VC Staff 30 VC Staff october 07 VC Staff

december 02 VC Staff 08 VC Staff 16 VC Staff **2016** january 13 VC

Staff 27 VC Staff may 11 VC Staff 18 VC DESIGN THINKING 23 VC DESIG

26 VC Staff november 02 VC Staff 09 VC Staff 09 DESIGN STUDIES 16 D

DESIGN STUDIES 15 VC staff 20 DESIGN STUDIES 22 VC staff 27 DESIGN

VC Staff 10 VC Stafff august 30 VC Staff 31 DESIGN STUDIES septem

DESIGN STUDIES october 03 DESIGN STUDIES 05 DESIGN STUDIES 11

02 DESIGN STUDIES 08 VC Staff 09 DESIGN STUDIES 15 VC Staff 16 DESIGN

17 VC Staff 24 VC Staff 31VC Staff february 07 VC Staff 14 VC Staff 21V

Staff 18 DESIGN STUDIES 25 VC Staff september 05 VC Staff 12 VC Staff

21 VC Staff 28 VC Staff december 05 VC Staff **2019** february 06

08 Final logistics DEDICATION october 07 MDESIGN STUDIES 28 MDESIGN STUDIES november 03 open VC

DESIGN STUDIES 17 open VC 18 MDESIGN STUDIES **2011** january 13 DESIGN STUDIES 20 DESIGN STUD-

17 DESIGN STUDIES 24 DESIGN STUDIES 31 DESIGN STUDIES april 07 DESIGN STUDIES 14 DESIGN STUDIES

DIES 19 DESIGN STUDIES 26 DESIGN STUDIES july 04 –17 DESIGN STUDIES Venice and London septem-

er 06 MSDESIGN STUDIES 13 MSDESIGN STUDIES 20 MSDESIGN STUDIES november 03 MSDESIGN STUD-

01 MFADESIGN STUDIES 07 VC staff 08 MFADESIGN STUDIES **2012** january 04 VC Staff 05 MFADESIGN

STUDIES february 01 VC Staff 02 MFADESIGN STUDIES 08 VC Staff 09 MFADESIGN STUDIES 15 VC Staff 16

MDESIGN STUDIES 29 VC planning april 05 VC planning 05 MDESIGN STUDIES 12 VC planning 12 MDESIGN

may 03 VC planning 03 MDESIGN STUDIES 10 VC planning 10 MDESIGN STUDIES september 05 VC Staff

DESIGN STUDIES october 03 VC Staff 04 MDESIGN STUDIES 10 VC Staff 11 MDESIGN STUDIES 17 VC Staff

01 MDESIGN STUDIES 07VC Staff 08 MDESIGN STUDIES 14 VC Staff 15 MDESIGN STUDIES december **2013**

06 VC Staff 13 VC Staff 20 VC Staff 27 VC Staff april 03 VC Staff 13 VC Staff 10 VC Staff 17 VC Staff may 01

DIES august 14 VC Staff 21 VC Staff 28 VC Staff september 04 VC Staff 11 VC Staff 18 VC Staff 25 VC

nber 06 VC Staff 13 VC Staff 20 VC Staff 27 VC Staff december 04 VC Staff 11 VC Staff 18 VC Staff **2014**

5 VC staff 05 VCDMDESIGN STUDIES 12 VCDMDESIGN STUDIES 19 VC Staff 19 VCDMDESIGN STUDIES 26

ESIGN STUDIES 19 VCDMDESIGN STUDIES 26 VC Staff 26 VCDMDESIGN STUDIES april 02 VC Staff 02 VCD-

IGN STUDIES 30 VC Staff 30 VCDMDESIGN STUDIES may 07 VC Staff 07 VCDMDESIGN STUDIES 14 VC Staff

ptember 11 VC Staff 18 VC Staff 25 VC Staff october 02 VC Staff 09 VC Staff 16 VC Staff 23 VC Staff 30 VC

Staff **2015** january 28 VC Staff february 04 VC Staff 11 Staff march 04 VC

Staff may 06 VC Staff 13 VC Staff VCDMDESIGN STUDI VC Staff septem-

21 VC Staff 27 VC Staff november 04 VC Staff 10 VC DIES 24 VC Staff

uary 10 VC Staff 24 VC Staff march 02 VC Staff 09 VC 13 VC Staff 20 VC

august 19 VC DESIGN THINKING 24 VC Staff septe ober 05 VC Staff

DIES december 07 VC Staff 14 VC Staff 14 DESIGN STUDIE staff 08 VC staff 13

march 01 VC staff 08 VC staff 22 VC Staff april 05 VC St 26 VC Staff may 03

Staff 07 DESIGN STUDIES 13 VC staff 14 DESIGN STUDIES 2 TUDIES 27 VC Staff 28

2 DESIGN STUDIES 18 VC Staff19 DESIGN STUDIES 25 VC Staff november 01 VC Staff

22 VC Staff 29 VC Staff 30 DESIGN STUDIES december 06 VC Staff 07 DESIGN STUDIES **2018** january

VC Staff march 07 VC staff 21 VC Staff 28 VC Staff april 04 VC Staff 04 DESIGN STUDIES 11 VC Staff 18 VC

26 VC Staff october 03 VC Staff 17 VC Staff 24 VC Staff 31 VC Staff november 07 VC Staff 14 VC Staff

Staff 20 VC Staff 27 VC staff march 06 VC staff 20 VC staff 27 VC staff april 03 VC staff 10 VC staff 17 VC staff

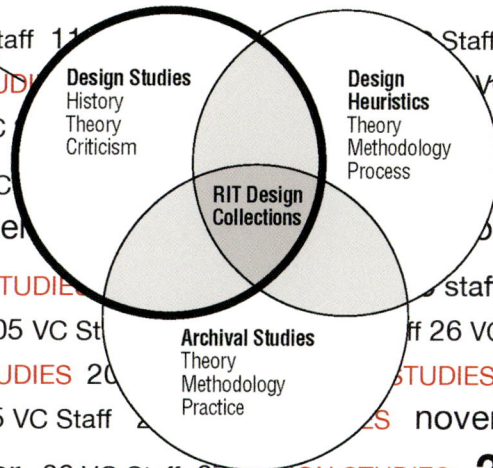

Design Studies
History
Theory
Criticism

Design Heuristics
Theory
Methodology
Process

RIT Design Collections

Archival Studies
Theory
Methodology
Practice

The Merging of Design and Business

Ken DeLor
RIT Graduate
President, DeLor Brand Identity
and Communications

Early in our design education, we are introduced to problem-solving methodology and how essential it is to establishing an objective process for creating visual communication solutions. But it was during my first design position in a Midwest manufacturing firm that an aha moment happened, changing the rest of my design life.

Working within the marketing group, I was introduced to a new concept in business planning, management by objectives, an approach to organizational management that brought a new and objective process to the world of business.

And there it was—the aha moment. This objective business approach had many of the same components as our own design methodology. And it fit like a glove. The merger of design and business had begun.

I spent the next five years with this company, learning the language of business and management by objectives while developing the corporate branding program. However, realizing the need for stronger visual control, I returned to graduate school at RIT and the mentorship of Roger Remington. Merging design methodology with the visual aesthetics proved to be the optimum combination for the next step.

A Strategic Marketing and Design Focus
When I eventually formed a design firm focused on branding, it became clear that the collaboration of strategic marketers and excellent designers was essential. While clients were looking for creative expertise, they thought branding was only a "creative exercise"—a feel-good moment for the artist and one of personal preference for the senior executive. Providing an objective process, which allowed clients the opportunity to participate in the program, was eye-opening and yet, ironically, familiar. Knowledge about the company/products, marketplace trends in the industry, competitive analysis, and program objectives/outcomes was now included in our methodology. New, however, was how to translate that knowledge into the power of a brand–brand positioning (strategy) and visual translation (design).

A Case Study in Diabetes

Working with pharmaceutical companies whose expertise is the treatment of diabetes proved to be more than just another project. Retained to create a comprehensive diabetes education program, we realized quickly that the first treatment of diabetes begins with patient education. It is the patient's first line of defense. And we found that while companies were spending millions of dollars developing diabetes educational materials, there was little connection between their corporate brand, products, or services.

Collaborating with diabetes educators, physicians, and client marketers over many months, we built a comprehensive, visually cohesive education program while helping clients establish a brand leadership position in the treatment of diabetes.

We were fortunate enough to produce similar programs, written in fifty languages, for diabetes patients throughout the world.

Diabetes Education Program
developed for Pfizer Pharmaceuticals
as the first line of treatment for diabetes
Photo by Michael Brohm Photography

From Dessau
to Rochester

Klaus Pollmeier
Nicolai Neubert
Professors
Dessau School of Design
Anhalt University of Applied Sciences

Dear Roger,
It is with our greatest pleasure that we use this opportunity to thank you for your enduring support of the Dessau School of Design at Anhalt University of Applied Sciences. Shortly after it was founded, you visited us—curious to find out what a design school would be like, if it was positioned next to and in the tradition of the Bauhaus. Your interest and advice were greatly appreciated, and we benefited a lot from your tremendous knowledge as designer and design historian. Without you, the wonderful student exchange program between RIT and Anhalt University would not exist.

Over time, your generous and unselfish personality made our relationship turn from professional respect and recognition into enduring friendship. To see that your greatest achievement—the Vignelli Center for Design Studies—developed from an idea and a sketch into a wonderfully built resource for students and scholars, makes us take our hats off. We look forward to learning more from you when you will lecture again on the Bauhaus stage in the hopefully not too distant future.

With highest respect and our best wishes for the future,

Nicolai Neubert and Klaus Pollmeier
Dessau School of Design
Anhalt University of Applied Sciences

Sketch of R. Roger Remington's office
by Massimo Vignelli
Photo by Nicolai Neubert

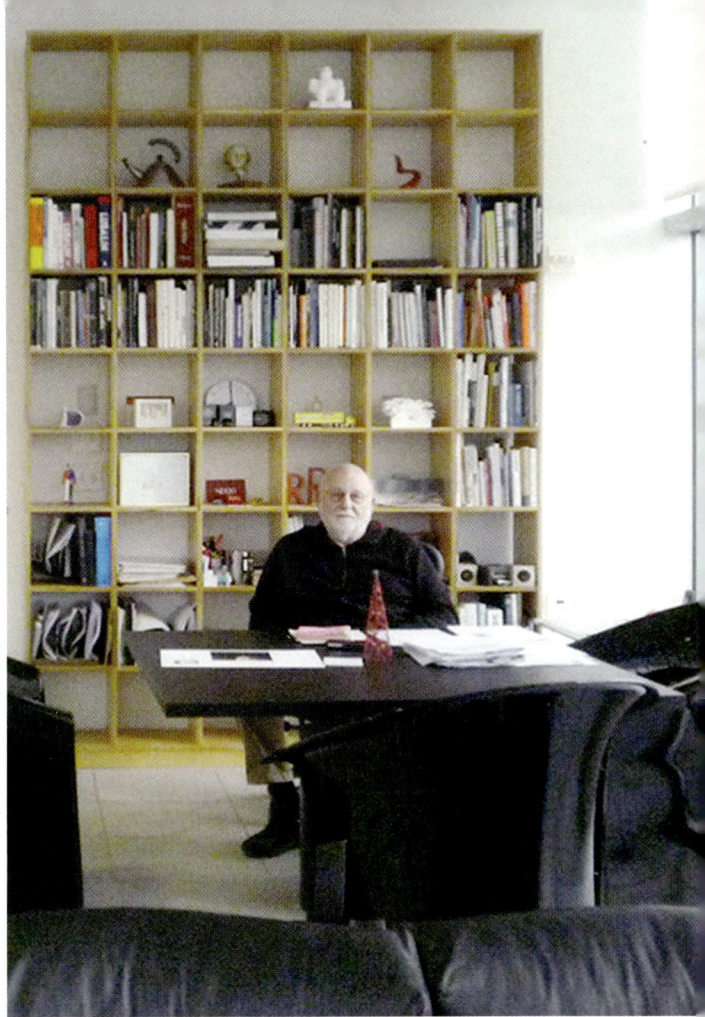

R. Roger Remington in his office, 2016
Photo by Nicolai Neubert

Exponential Impact

Lee Green
RIT Masters Graduate, 1974
RIT College of Imaging Arts and Sciences

We seldom realize the exponential impact we have, impact that extends far beyond a single individual, but then from that individual to their subsequent influence on cities, countries, businesses, and many other people.

Such is the case with Roger Remington's impact on me—and then my ability to leverage everything I was taught at RIT as I moved through life.

After I graduated with a Master's degree from RIT's design program, Roger recommended me to the City of Rochester, NY. The City had received a grant from the National Endowment for the Arts to develop a two-year city identity and design program. I took that job and went on to create what was essentially a corporate identity program for a city. I've managed to locate some examples of publications along with the city mark I designed, which is still in use today. I'd like to think the impact of that effort will extend into the future as well.

City mark first introduced on the 1976 City of Rochester Annual Report Photo by Lee Green

Five years later, I was still working as the City's designer when Roger got a call from IBM in San Jose, California. They were looking for a designer and had reached out to several universities. Roger once again recommended me. I flew off to California with my portfolio. IBM hired me as a junior designer, and I moved to California. After about five years, I mentioned to my boss that I might like to work for IBM on the east coast, closer to IBM headquarters. He said it just so happened IBM was starting up a new business and product in Boca Raton, Florida, and wanted to know if I'd be interested in relocating there. I asked what the product was. He said he thought it was called a personal computer.

Long story short, I went on to become IBM's Chief Designer and Corporate Vice President with global responsibility for all of IBM's identity, branding, industrial design, web design, divestitures, etc.

One of the many, and perhaps most enjoyable, projects of my thirty-seven year career with IBM was the design and production of IBM's centennial anniversary exhibition at Lincoln Center. That exhibition went on and traveled to Epcot Center, the Chicago Museum of Science and Industry, and the Fort Worth Museum of Science and History.

Several years ago, I was also honored by RIT as a Distinguished Alumnus.

There is no way I can express sufficient gratitude to RIT, but particularly to Roger Remington. He made learning design a wonderful experience. And his mentorship has changed many lives for the better. Not just the lives of his students, but the lives of everyone and everything those students went on to influence.

My sincere congratulations, Roger, on a wonderful career. Wishing you the very best.

Lee Green
Wake Forest, NC

THINK: An exploration into making
the world work better
Exhibit at Lincoln Center, NYC
IBM centennial, 2011
Photo courtesy of Lee Green

Roger Remington
Brings It Home

Lorraine Justice
PHD, FIDSA, Dean Emerita
Professor of Industrial Design, RIT

One of Roger's biggest legacies at RIT is certainly the Vignelli Center for Design Studies. It is a testament to the contributions of the Vignellis' lifetime of work, and it is also a testament to the lifetime of the work of Roger. You see, he didn't just make the Vignellis' work come alive on the RIT campus; he brought in the work of other designers as well. In the Vignelli Center are the following collections: Massimo and Lella Vignelli Papers, Unimark International Records, Arnold Saks Papers, RitaSue Siegel Records, Michael Bierut Posters, Armando Milani Posters, Robert Appleton Papers, Joe A. Watson Posters, Kodak 1939 World's Fair Letters, and a time capsule of work with collections from Wendell Castle, Cory Grosser, and Josh Owen.

Roger didn't stop there. In fact, he had started collecting archives for RIT thirty years earlier. There is another fabulous archive collection at the RIT Wallace Library in the Cary Graphic Design Archive. This collection holds samples from forty-five designers and typographers from the United States and Canada:

Dr. Mehemed Fehmy Agha
Walter Allner
Hans J. Barschel
Saul Bass
Herbert Bayer
Lester Beall
Ed Benguiat
Alexey Brodovitch
Will Burtin
Tom Carnese
Chermayeff and Geismar
Elaine Lustig Cohen
Charles Coiner
Henrietta Condak
Louis Danziger
Rudolph de Harak
Lou Dorfsman
Mary Faulconer
Gene and Helen Federico
George Giusti
William Golden
Rolf Harder

Ken Hiebert
E. McKnight Kauffer
Rob Roy Kelly
Burton Kramer
Willi Kunz
Mo Lebowitz
Matthew Leibowitz
Leo Lionni
Pippo Lionni
Alvin Lustig
Tomoko Miho
Joyce Morrow
Cipe Pineles
Paul Rand
Estelle Ellis Rubinstein
Alex Steinweiss
Ladislav Sutnar
Ceil Smith Thayer
Bradbury Thompson
Fred Troller
George Tscherny

The contributions of these archives are many: students use them for inspiration for design projects, faculty use them for their research, and visitors from around the world come to visit these archives, which will only grow in value and importance.

Yes, it was Roger's great foresight to start collecting the work of other designers and to have those archives be "working archives," where students and researchers can see firsthand the beauty, intelligence, and craft of great designers and typographers. Thank you, Roger.

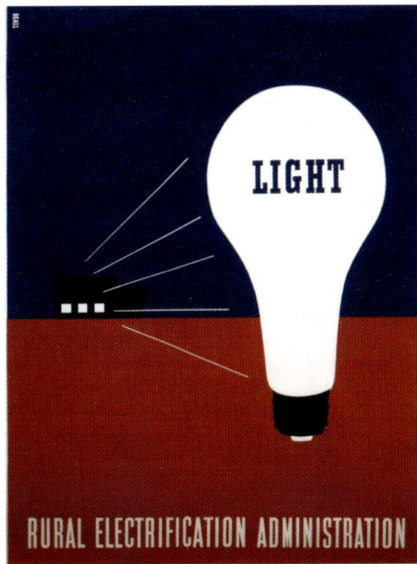

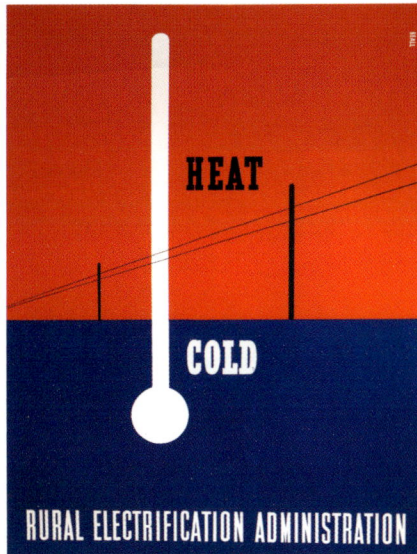

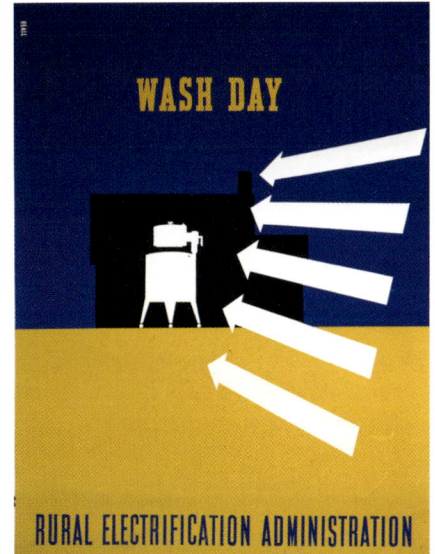

Top, left:
Light *poster by Lester Beall*

Bottom, left:
Heat Cold *poster by Lester Beall*

Top, right:
Farm Work *poster by Lester Beall*

Bottom, right:
Wash Day *poster by Lester Beall*

RIT
Hope for Honduras

Mary Golden
M.arch., NCIDQ Assistant Professor
Undergraduate Program Director
RIT Interior Design
Director RIT Hope for Honduras

The RIT *Hope for Honduras* initiative aims to support efforts to reduce infant mortality by improving access to quality medical care and educational services through design innovation. The goal of the multidisciplinary collective is to foster an exchange of knowledge from areas of divergent expertise to transform mother and infant care in the country of Honduras. Hope for Honduras research investigations place emphasis on public good by fostering agency and self-reliance in human-centered design-build projects that address critical global issues and advance the right of every person to live in a socially, economically, and environmentally just community.

The holistic, inclusive approach to experiential field and studio-based research promotes the discovery of innovative, socially relevant designs with potential as scalable microenterprise solutions. Grounded in the principles of universal design, human factors explorations advance prototype research to create healing types of architecture and interior environments while inspiring global citizenry in university students.

Right, top:
Mary Golden, RIT Hope For Honduras, and Christian Perry, Little Angels of Honduras at WantedDesign 2018, Brooklyn, NY Photo by Christian Perry

Right, middle:
Students departing for the five-day RIT Hope for Honduras trip

Right, bottom:
RIT Hope for Honduras introduced to RITchie the Tiger!

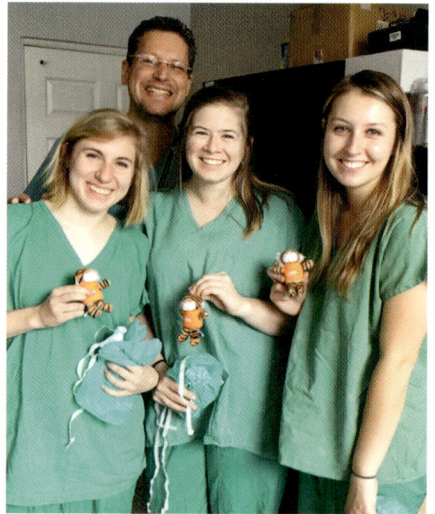

Above:
Conducting research at Hospital Escuela
All photos by Mary Golden

Right:
Variations developed by R. Roger
Remington and Bruce Ian Meader for a
typographic, parent-child identity

R·I·T
Hope for
Honduras

Little Angels
of
Honduras

Skin to Skin
Incubation

Roger Remington
at Università Iuav di Venezia

Medardo Chiapponi
Educator, Full Professor of Design
Università Iuav di Venezia

I have, and with me the international design community has, several reasons to be grateful to Roger Remington. I'd like to remember a couple of them–other people will illuminate different facets of his multiple contributions as a designer, design theorist and historian, educator, research and education promoter, and manager.

My first reason for appreciation, before meeting him personally, is what I have learned from his books (especially interesting for me has been *Design and Science*), where Roger, thanks to his thorough historical research work, opens innovative approaches to contemporary and future design.

Later I had a key opportunity to be with him from the beginning in the network *MEDdesign*, dealing with medical design and involving, in addition to RIT Vignelli Center for Design Studies and Università Iuav di Venezia, Technion-Israel Institute of Technology, Helen Hamlyn Centre for Design at Royal College of Art, and Sheffield Hallam University. The *MEDdesign* conference held in Rochester, organized by Roger, and the one in London have deepened important questions concerning health, well-being, the role of design in promoting the best solutions in these fields, and the ability to do it in cooperation with other disciplines and professional skills. A good example of the output of the *MEDdesign* activity at Vignelli Center is the demonstration project "Human Health" developed by teams of graduate graphic design students coordinated by Bruce Ian Meader together with Roger and published in 2013.

Another milestone (not in chronological order) is the inspiring didactic approach of the international Master of Arts in Integrated Design (MAID) at Anhalt University, Dessau, located in the Bauhaus building, which Roger contributed to enormously, together with Joachim Krausse and Michael Burke. Roger was teaching Information Design, and this connects with another experience I have shared with him and on which I'd like to focus in my homage.

Roger Remington with students in Murano
Photo by Medardo Chiapponi

I am referring to the one-week workshop Roger held with our design students: an exciting experience for everyone who had the chance to participate, and one that left deep traces on the improvement of our program. The goal of research and development performed by the students was an integrated set of promotional posters about Murano to communicate information to a general audience. Students were required to use a rational, objective, systematic approach to problem-solving. The key strategy for the project was to maintain simplicity, be organized, and place priority on making complex information clear and coherent. The class was organized in four working teams, each with a different information theme:

- Identity program and graphic standards for posters
- Orientation to Murano
- Murano yesterday
- Murano today

Roger's evaluation of the results was: "The students had been very serious, dedicated and professional about their responsibilities. The final poster series evidenced concern for information hierarchy, consistency and overall excellence as the deliverables met and exceeded the workshop goals."

It was thanks to you, Roger!

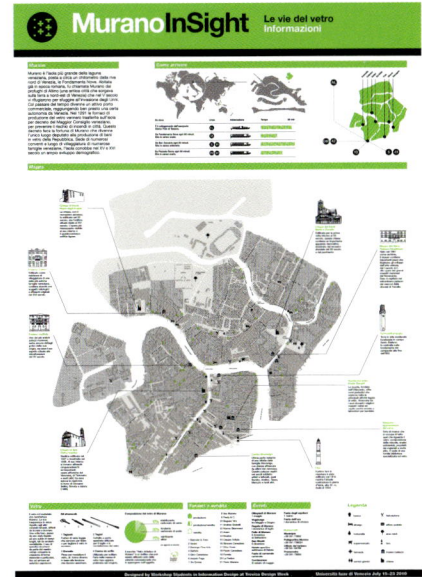

Murano city promotional posters, 2010
Designed by students of Visiting Professor R. Roger Remington

Meredith Davis
Professor Emerita
Department of Graphic and
Industrial Design
College of Design, NC State University

Graphic Design:
From Trade to Profession

Modern design professions arose from the trades of printing, handcraft, and building. Guilds dedicated to these vocations flourished in Europe as early as the twelfth century and required instrumental know-how for membership; practical reasoning about what worked best in a particular medium or context. Historically, novices acquired such knowledge through apprenticeships under experienced masters and through trial and error in concrete situations.

Circumstances of the twentieth century transformed design trades into design professions. Mass production presented new demands for volume, standardization, efficiency, and profitability not easily met by cottage industries. Unlike the improvisational work of individual craftsmen, these efforts required analysis, planning, and coordination.

Industry deepened its reliance on statistical insights as schools of management imported theories from the social sciences and cast business as a system of inputs, transformation processes, and outputs. And as the quantitative differences among competing products narrowed, companies realized they needed to know something about the qualitative preferences of consumers to succeed. By the middle of the century, design played a critical role in this increasingly complex system.

During this period, technological leadership moved from Europe to the United States where, free from the ravages of war, there was continuing capacity for innovation and potential for converting it to marketable opportunities. On the heels of the Manhattan Project, universities shifted their priorities from basic research to solving the complex problems of society, and opening the door for new academic programs with practical goals, including design.

Although American industry was known for its technical expertise, the immigration of European design faculty provided universities with new intellectual resources for developing a professional workforce in modern design.

All true professions, including design, exhibit behaviors not found in trades. Professionals show an intellectual interest in methods and challenge their effectiveness under changing conditions. In the 1960s and 1970s, the study of design methods was a focus in a number of schools, most notably the Ulm School of Design. And today, there are graduate design programs devoted exclusively to methodological issues and the work of interdisciplinary teams resulting from the expanding scope of design problems.

Professions have codes of ethics that are frequently articulated by professional associations and debated by the community of practice as surrounding conditions change. For many years, this professional code had more to do with how designers should be treated than with the consequences of design for people and the environment. But in recent years, human-centered and social design practices have turned professional attention to issues beyond the short-term satisfaction of client desires for profit and standards of fair practice.

And as the rapid growth of digital technology undermines traditional assumptions about *privacy*, *authorship*, and even *truth*, audiences for design consistently choose honesty and doing good things for the world over cleverness and invention.

Unlike trades, professions engage in critical discourse and research. Through conferences and writing, they actively critique the work of practitioners and scholars. They project future conditions that are likely to shape responses by the field. Professions have segments of practice dedicated solely to the generation of new knowledge. An emerging research culture—supported by recent research-based doctoral design programs in several American universities—is dedicated to the development of theories and findings with broad application to the practice and discipline. These programs examine how designers think; what people want and need; what the context demands; how design is planned, produced, and distributed; consequences of design action; and methods for studying these things. Graduates make important contributions to the growing number of firms engaged in design research and offer new forms of faculty scholarship as alternatives to artistic practice in colleges and universities.

Professions document their histories in literature that interprets the work of practitioners within the context of surrounding conditions and events. Unlike other design fields, the history of graphic design was slow to develop. Although there were several comprehensive chronologies of graphic design written in the early 1980s, they largely mirrored the history of fine art, especially in Europe and even when arts movements began through the design of texts. AIGA, the professional association for the discipline, archived work from its annual competitions but provided little interpretation of the work, organizing it largely by format until much later when work from 1980 to 2012 was transferred to the Denver Art Museum.

Roger Remington at Rochester Institute of Technology took the lead in developing American graphic design history. He worked tirelessly to acquire the work of modernist designers, now housed in the Cary Graphic Arts Collection. This collection of forty-five designers' work provides a coherent view of midcentury modernism in the United States, making it a primary-source treasure for historians of the period. First on a laser disc of nearly ten thousand images, and eventually in a professionally managed collection accessible to scholars, the archive supported research for a number of important texts, as well as Roger's seminal writing.

It is impossible to over-estimate Roger's early 1980s insight in collecting objects that had yet to gain broad recognition and studying a period that was pivotal in the professional maturation of the field. He then extended the intellectual reach of RIT's modernist holdings to include product design through the unparalleled bequests of Massimo and Lella Vignelli in the Vignelli Center for Design Studies. The curatorial coherence of RIT acquisitions is further reflected in Roger Remington's books. While early graphic design chronologies by others were essential in defining the breadth of the field, Roger offered historiographic exemplars for a maturing profession through biographical depth and contextual analysis. He taught others how to do design history.

In a recent interview, I was asked to describe the difference between training and education. I responded that training involves the transfer of settled knowledge with the goal of student *proficiency*. On the other hand, education is transformative; it challenges a worldview, confirming or recalibrating individual beliefs, values, and ways of thinking. Its goal is *insight*. Trades seek proficiency; professions seek more. The relationship between a design student and faculty is not one of apprentice and master, as it is commonly described; it is one of conversation and active inquiry in an ongoing search for meaningful patterns. This book honors a professional life dedicated to that relationship.

A Great Pleasure
to Have
Worked with You

Michael Burke
Vignelli Center Visiting Scholar
Graphic Design Educator
Historian, Author, Design Collector

The name R. Roger Remington is synonymous with the RIT School of Design and the Cary Graphic Design Archive at RIT.

He has succeeded (together with the late Massimo Vignelli) in creating the outstanding collection of not only American but international examples of graphic design. It is quite unique and is indispensable for future generations of history of design students, as well as a resource that Roger uses in his undergraduate and graduate lectures.

He has acquired an abundant enthusiasm for and knowledge of design over the years with his many contacts and European travels. I first discovered Roger through his book *Nine Pioneers in American Graphic Design* (1989), but I was to meet him personally during my time as Professor for Design at the Fachhochschule for Gestaltung Schwäbisch Gmünd in Germany.

I believe Roger was invited to give a series of design history lectures there and I invited him to attend my intermediate critique in my Concept Design Development, Type and Image class. In just a few days, it became clear that we shared the same interest in design history, modernism, and information design.

Over the years we were to meet in various locations, notably in the newly formed Masters program (MAID) at the Anhalt University, Dessau. This was in the original Bauhaus complex where I was teaching with Dr. Joachim Krausse. It was a magic moment for me to be in this historic building. Roger and I were teaching the same group of Information Design students. During this period, as part of a student excursion, we visited the excellent Ladislav Sutnar exhibition in Prague. In 2000, I was guest information design editor for the magazine *Graphics International* and invited Roger to contribute an article on the American designer Will Burtin.

I have been privileged to be invited twice to RIT as a Vignelli Visiting Scholar to work with Roger, his colleagues, and their students. I gave various lectures and was involved with individual projects, including the Vignelli Center's initiative, *MEDdesign*, focused on inclusive design for human needs in a medical context. I collaborated with Roger and Dr. Medardo Chiapponi from the University of Venice. Over the years, we have met at various conferences linked to the medical design project, notably in London.

Medardo also invited me to work with his students on two interface design projects. Roger and I were able to meet again, when he was working with a group of students on an information design poster project for Murano. This allowed us to discuss new developments and, of course, enjoy the local gastronomy!

It has been a great pleasure to have worked with you.

Michael Burke worked with designer Otl Aicher to create graphics for the 1972 Olympics in Munich Germany. He subsequently donated 26 Olympic posters to the Vignelli Center for Design Studies.

Above:
Michael Burke critiquing student work at RIT

Right:
Olympicvision poster
Advanced Information Design class RIT
topic: 2012 London Olympics
Diagrams, flag icons, photographs, isotype symbols, and maps compare data for the 3 times London hosted the Olympics: 1908, 1948, and 2012
Design by Brittany Schlunt, 2012

Photo and image this page courtesy of Bruce Ian Meader

A Unity of Opposites

Michael Taylor
Former Head of the Glass Department
College of Imaging Arts and Sciences, RIT

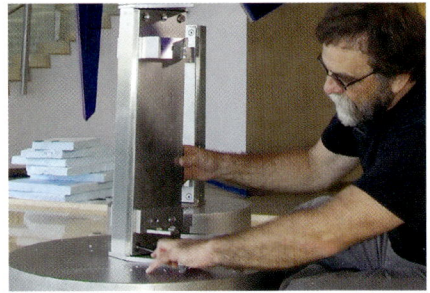

Michael Taylor installing Cadence, *a glass and stainless steel sculpture*
Photo by Matt Silk

Catalog for A Unity of Opposites, Recent Work by Michael Taylor, 2009
Design by R. Roger Remington and Bruce Ian Meader

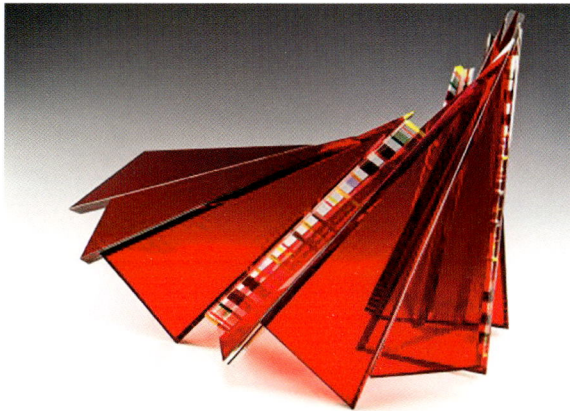

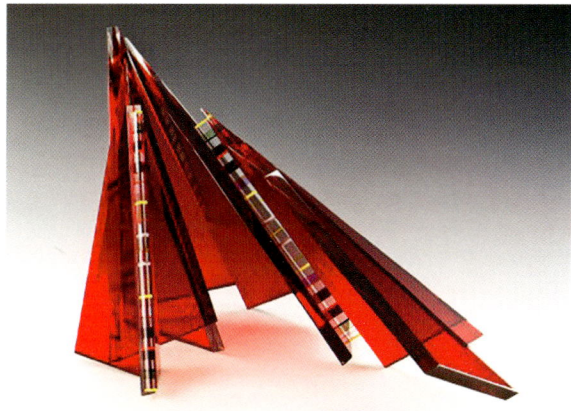

Clockwise:
Cloak and Dagger *(two views), 2010*
Ascending Spiral, *20 x 29 inches*
Synoptic Torsion *series, detail*
Photos by Bruce Miller

Shaping an Experience and Making Connections

Peter Byrne
Educator, Professor, School Director
School of Design, RIT

Over twenty years ago, I joined the Graphic Design program as a new faculty member, and was fortunate enough to share my first office with Roger. Generous and welcoming, Roger immediately made me feel at home. Initially I was driving back and forth from Buffalo, New York, and upon hearing this, Roger handed me his card and said that if I ever needed a place to stay, his door was always open to me. This gracious act typifies Roger's way of living and working: generous and openhearted to all.

With a big heart, a robust laugh, and never at a loss for a historical connection, Roger has been a part of my daily life as a faculty member in the School of Design. During his fifty-seven year career at RIT, Roger has shaped generations of designers, educators, and scholars with his passion for design. It is natural for him to support those around him. I only had to mention that I was teaching a class new to me and he would offer up numerous resources and helpful hints for success.

An aspect of Roger's life that is not as well known is his history as a printmaker. Talented with form, shape, line, and color, Roger created works that were playful, vibrant, and intellectually engaging. Roger's deep inquiry into all things design began with the rigor of his own visual exploration. Lively compositions exploring harmony, tension, and relationships, his creative work holds your attention. Roger's energetic thirst for learning and sharing knowledge starts with those prints and collages, and continues through to his scholarly impact on graphic design.

Roger has worked tirelessly to build an impactful legacy of teaching and learning about design. To educate is to foster and nurture, and to provide intellectual nourishment. With his inquisitiveness and enthusiasm for design, Roger is an educator who learns as much as he teaches. In conversations with Roger, I am always amazed at his ability to make connections with the past that are so very integral to our current times. Keenly aware of the evolving field of design, Roger is excited about the future, and his energy and positive outlook is refreshing and much needed. Leading a dynamic and full life, Roger has always made time to share a laugh, a story, and many times much-needed wisdom. Roger has indeed ushered hundreds of us along, bequeathing his passion and excitement for design, and teaching us about living a life full of purpose.

Opposite:
Peter Byrne, Legacy
Oil on YUPO paper, 14 x 11 inches

The Seeds of Design Knowledge

Petra Mueller-Csernetzky
Educator, Professor University of Applied Sciences Lucerne, Visiting Professor University of Applied Sciences Dessau New Design University St. Pölten, Södertörn, University Stockholm

I first met R. Roger Remington in 2003 as a student of the international master's program Integrated Design in Dessau. In his role as visiting professor, he was able to offer central insights into information design through his lectures. At that time, this was an absolute enrichment against the background of the emerging wave of digitalization with the possibilities of data visualization. Especially as first-year students, working with him opened our eyes, and we got to know the difference between data, information, and knowledge in the context of design. Excursions to Prague, Berlin, Cologne, or Frankfurt, including exhibitions on Will Burtin or Roger's work on Lester Beall, completed the profile of a designer who is nourished by the examination of complex questions but always combines a transformation of information with the useful-visible. A truly modernist attitude.

It became clear that in the work of numerous designers throughout history, this attitude has been a motivating force for their creative drive. I was able to broaden this insight with the master workshop for graphic designers, *Dialogues in Design*, on the French Riviera with Massimo Vignelli and Armando Milani in 2008. Our work there on visual language and expression showed once again that there are no limits to this kind of transformation. The iterative form-finding process of information and even knowledge can be transferred to the visual and haptic, but also to more abstract levels like a corporate strategy. The visual appearance, the corporate design, then becomes a symbol and indicator for identity and culture.

My understanding of the form-finding process has been constantly expanded through constructive discussions with Roger and visits to the Vignelli Center for Design Studies. Against the background of the development of design thinking, the fundamental understanding of visualization has established itself as a widely used method in product and service development, both within and outside the design world. The work of designers, in innovative projects of various kinds, has its roots in the first insights of design as a discipline. In design research, these issues have been addressed by researchers such as Nigel Cross, Donald Schön, and Richard Buchanan.

In particular, the skill of making the hidden visible has long been a topic of art theory, not only since modernism. But it first had to be recognized as a core competence of design, although practice has proven this for a long time.

Today we no longer question the achievements of design in the private sector because we know that these central achievements are useful. Understanding a customer's journey from different perspectives no longer seems to be an extraordinary challenge, especially when using virtual tools. Design is becoming larger and is expanding its horizons. However, practice shows bloomers, but also plants with a healthy structure. Even in hitherto unknown regions of the industry, one can now find an understanding of design with its verifiable qualities.

What was once considered a revelation about information design in the perception of my own career has now grown into a major achievement in the field—a growing capacity for cross-disciplinary thinking and action, throughout and beyond the design community. Roger had made us fit for the future at that time and helped design culture to flourish with his everlasting contribution.

All this has influenced and still does support me in my own lecturing practice. With the highest respect and gratefulness to Roger for this first impulse and all the years of constant care—*Onward*.

Opposite, left to right:
Various impressions: Dessau (2003);
Nice (2008); Briey (2010); Lauchheim (2015)

This page:
Lake Ontario (2019)
All photos by Petra Mueller-Csernetzky

Preservation

Philip Burton
Founding Chair and Professor in
Graphic Design, School of Design,
University of Illinois at Chicago

Opposite:
*My afternoon arrival at RIT started
immediately with a podcast—my first—
conducted by Roger Remington and
Anne Ghory-Goodman with an emphasis
on questions about my Basel education.
The 4:45 p.m. presentation, "From
Mauerstrasse to Wall Street: A Designer's
Journey," went off without a hitch. Then
dinner with the faculty, a quick drink
and chat with Roger, and some sleep.
Early next morning it was off again to
an impromptu presentation to graduate
students. Roger had found some work
from my school days that he thought
would be interesting to explain. Outside
the window I could see the snow very
quickly building up. With some urgency,
Roger drove me to the airport. I caught
the last plane out of the airport and I was
on my way back to Chicago.*

As a student at the School of Design in Basel, Switzerland, I was invited to design all the print material—poster, invitation, signage, envelopes, etc.—for the ATypI (Paris-based Association Typographique Internationale) First Working Seminar: Education in Letterforms, Signs and Symbols held at the School of Design in November 1974. Because of that work, I was invited to design the article about the seminar that appeared in Typographische Monatsblätter a year later. I had to deliver the mechanicals for the article to the editor, Rudolf Hostettler, in St. Gallen.

It was an honor for me to meet Herr Hostettler, a person whom I considered to have been of considerable importance in the history of Swiss typography. Herr Hostettler was working on an issue devoted to the work of friend and colleague Jan Tschichold, who had died a year earlier. He had just received a package of Tschichold's work from his widow, Edith. When he opened the package and spread the work out on the table, I was stunned. I was certainly familiar with Tschichold's work, but only through reproductions in books. But here it was, the real stuff.

I learned what I thought was an important lesson that day. (I know this sounds naive.) No reproduction can compare to seeing the original size, paper quality, ink coverage, even the smell of an original piece of work.

My first visit to RIT was to join the celebration of the opening of the Vignelli Center for Design Studies, a sleek steel and glass structure that houses a one-of-a-kind archive. Huge sliding walls and flat files hold artifacts, samples, models, and what looks like every piece of paper touched by Lella and Massimo Vignelli. The labels on the flat file drawers have numbers penciled in by Mr. Vignelli himself. The typeface is Bodoni. A small gallery space is devoted to key works that document the significance of the Vignelli design studio. This is work that helped shape the development of design in America and around the world. Many pieces are deftly sketched in pencil for proposed publications. All original work. An original New York subway map is particularly beautiful seen in person.

Being invited to RIT means podcast,
public presentation, dinner with
the faculty, late night drinks and design
conversation, some sleep, a morning
presentation to graduate students. What's
that accumulating outside? Snow!
Get me to the airport to catch the last
plane home.

Rocco Piscatello
Principal
Piscatello Design Centre

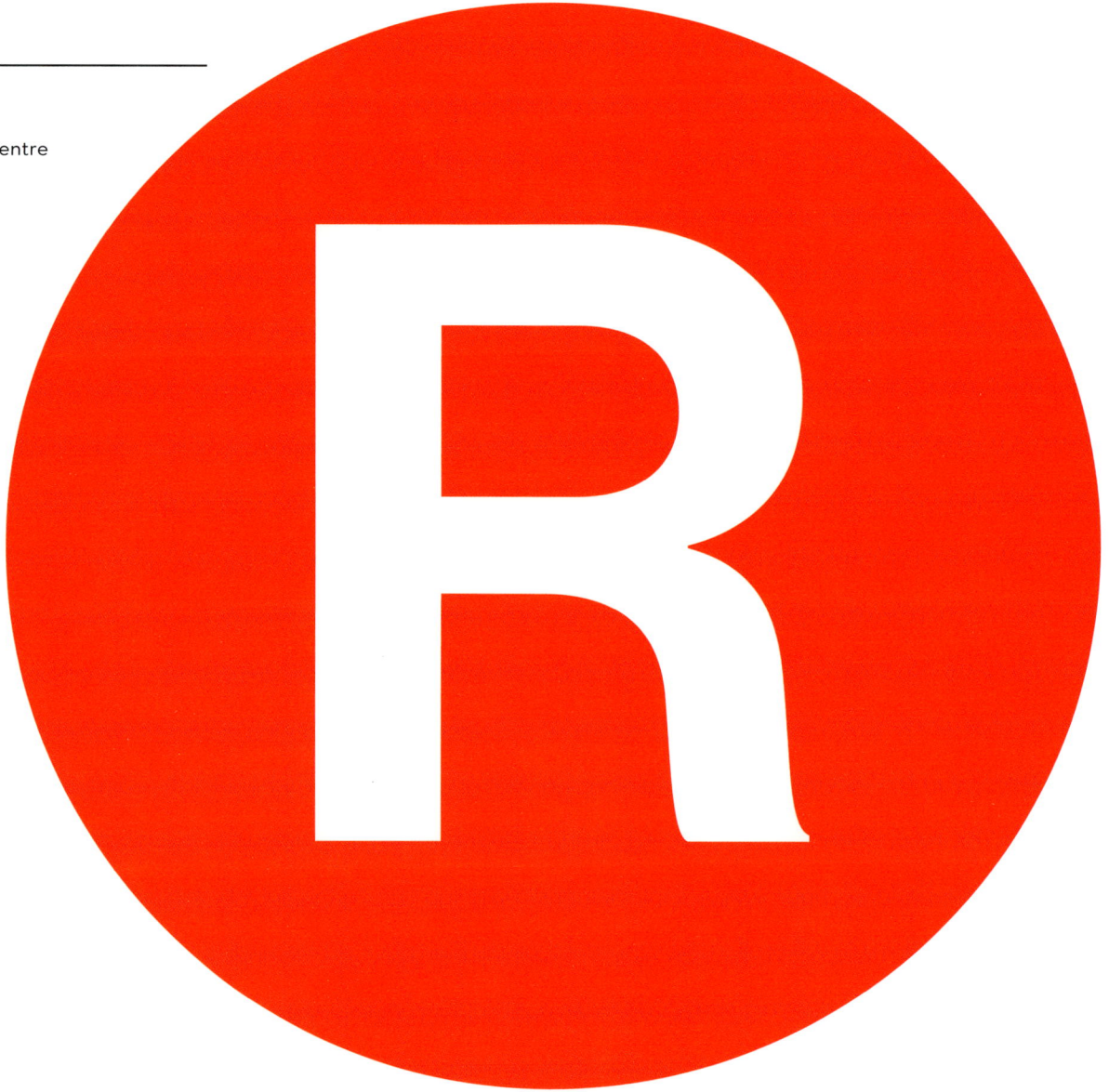

Planned Service Change

R. Roger Remington
Vignelli Distinguished Professor

Rochester Institute of Technology
From 1963 through 2020

Although Roger Remington has been teaching at RIT for fifty-seven years, it still feels like he is leaving too soon. RIT needs him; his students need him; we all need him. The world over will always need Roger.

What students receive from a great educator is not instruction but a demonstration of that person's view on life—a way of perceiving the world. Roger's total commitment to design is inspiring to all who know him.

Roger's scholarly action to collect the archives from the world's best graphic designers was a heroic one. With great foresight and tenacity, Roger has gifted future generations with invaluable resources from which to learn.

Lella and Massimo Vignelli aspired to create works that would be useful past their lifetimes. The best quality of the archives is that they will be used as a teaching device where students can learn and observe the work of master designers. The archives serve as a vehicle to show students what they cannot see.

Roger's vision has undoubtedly made a significant contribution to RIT and the world of design.

I congratulate Roger on his success and wish him the best in all the new ventures that life has in store for him.

With great admiration,
Rocco Piscatello

April 2020

New York

Photocomposing

Ryszard Horowitz
Photocomposer

Photocomposing is the best way to describe what I do. It is very similar to what a composer of music does in putting unrelated sounds into a coherent, harmonious and lucid piece. I assemble together my seemingly unrelated images, taken at different times, in distant parts of the world and create seamless compositions. I want all the elements to appear in the same space frozen in time.

I was trained as a painter and realized that I was more interested in making pictures rather than taking them. I began to paint images that were fantasy driven as opposed to realistic or naturalistic. Early on in my career I thought about all the possibilities for combining photos together. Frequently my work, done years before computers were used for imaging, is assumed to be digitally assembled.

Invitation from a retrospective exhibition at the Vignelli Center for Design Studies organized by R. Roger Remington, 2016 Design by Bruce Ian Meader

I've always looked for inspiration from great masters. I basically discovered everything I wanted to learn about composition and lighting from painters such as Caravaggio and Rembrandt. I looked to Mantegna for his perspective, admired the color of Picasso and Mattise and attempted to absorb a sense of whimsy from Magritte and Klee.

I consider digital imaging of today a magnificent tool that has made it possible for me to explore my visual ideas and has helped me to consolidate my love of painting with photography.

Opposite, clockwise:
Allegory *(1992)*
Nedda *(1969)*
Waterscape *(2006)*
Warsaw Ghetto Uprising *(2008)*
Wild Geese *(2016)*
Pearly Hand *(1971)*
Pinky Ring *(1973)*
Photocompositions by Ryszard Horowitz

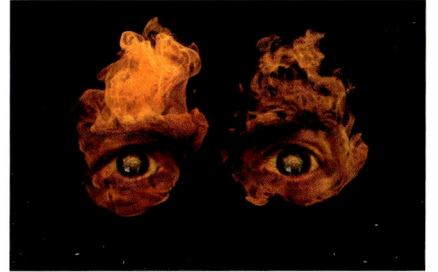

Design is one
Heroes, two

Sean Wolcott
Graphic Designer

July 2011—I was there! Finally, I made it to meet my design hero, Massimo Vignelli, at the newly opened Vignelli Center for Design Studies at RIT. It was beyond exciting and surreal. Quickly, though, as the events were under way, I realized there was another key force here—the warm, gracious, knowledgeable, and insightful talents of Roger Remington. But that was just the beginning.
Over that week and the years to come, I came to experience this passion and encouragement from two key people without whom my design and career would be much less.

It is clear how much Roger has not only a deep love for design but also compassion for the people behind it. And the same could easily be said of Massimo for Roger. Massimo, though vibrant and warm, was not one to be won over quickly. He clearly was for Roger, though, and you could see his admiration in all things. At RIT in 2012, I fondly remember presenting a design proposal to Massimo. In his state of excitement, the first thing proclaimed was, "Roger, get over here. You have to see this!" That excitement for design I take with me, and these two people I have most to thank for it.

Editorial graphic, 8 x 8 inches, 2020
Design by Sean Wolcott

Design is one
Heroes, two

Writing Histories

Sharon Poggenpohl
Educator, Editor
Editor Emerita, *Visible Language*

Around 1983 or 1984, when few people had access to individual email accounts, using his good offices, Roger arranged for me to get an email account at RIT. He was in New York and I was in Pennsylvania—he was writing something for *Visible Language* and I was the guest editor, so the quicker connection was useful. It was not until a decade later that I had my own academic account at IIT. He was early to understand the practical beauty of email and **generous** to share access with me.

I asked Roger how he was so productive with writing. He quietly told me he got up early, 5 or 6 am, as I recall, and worked on whatever book was on his mind. He also used idle fifteen-minute spaces in the day to write or review. That is how he kept ideas fresh in his mind and made progress on his project in a **disciplined** way. I wish I had such discipline.

He was instrumental in organizing, in 1983, *The First Symposium on the History of Graphic Design* at RIT. This was followed by a second symposium in 1985 and predated his book in 1989, *Nine Pioneers in American Graphic Design*. There wasn't much attention to history then. Roger himself was a pioneer. What courses existed crammed all design together—architectural, graphic, product, etc.—into a rapid-fire survey with little depth. Roger took another approach and gave us *Lester Beall* in 1996 and *Will Burtin* in 2009. And there were other books, some done collaboratively. He made us conscious of our history in an **accessible** and informative way.

At a time when serious history was a curiosity in graphic design, Roger set his course to change things. His **scholarship** set a standard for others. Art historians are abundant, but those who take design history seriously remain few. Roger leaves a **legacy** that we hope others will follow and extend his work.

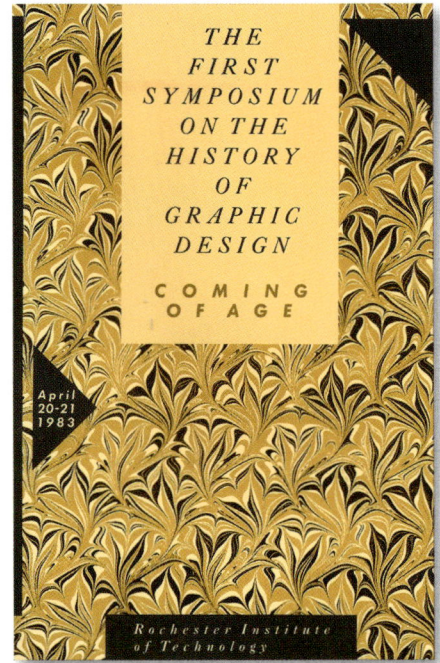

Above:
Publication with selected content from The First Symposium on the History of Graphic Design: Coming of Age Design by Heinz Klinkon, 1983

Opposite, top:
"Computer Graphics: What Do They Mean and How Do They Fit?," Visible Language 19, no. 2 (April 1985): 188–89, spread detail

Opposite, bottom:
"Computer Graphics: What Do They Mean and How Do They Fit?," Visible Language 19, no. 2 (April 1985): 179, spread detail

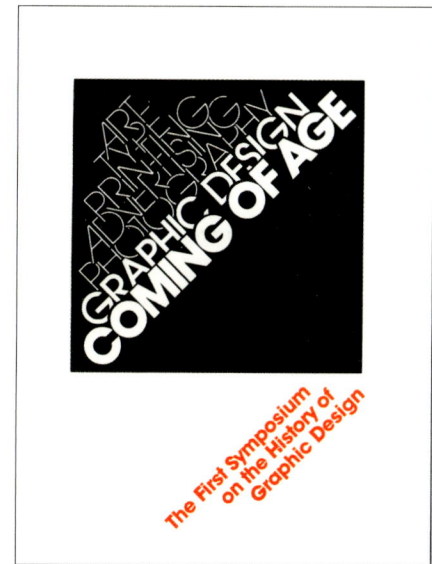

Above:
The First Symposium on the History of Graphic Design: Coming of Age Conference materials notebook Design by Scott Pipitone, 1983

Pioneering Design Education through the Graphic Design Archive

Steven Galbraith
Curator, RIT Cary Graphic Arts Collection

Dear Roger,

Decades ago, you recognized that the process work of graphic designers—their ephemeral sketches, paste-ups, photographs, and models—were invaluable teaching tools that revealed creative minds at work. With this in mind, you set out on a pioneering effort to collect this at-risk material and preserve it at RIT, where it could be consulted by students and researchers. Supported by, and later partnering with, Cary Curator David Pankow, you established the Graphic Design Archive (GDA), which has blossomed into an unparalleled archive representing forty-five significant graphic designers.

Now held in the Cary Graphic Arts Collection, the contents of the GDA are viewed by thousands of students each year, are reproduced in books and journals, and are loaned to exhibitions across the globe. In this way, although influential designers such as Cipe Pineles, George Giusti, Lester Beall, Elaine Lustig Cohen, and Will Burtin have passed on,

their creative work lives on to instruct and inspire new generations. This continued conversation was made possible by your vision and labor.

This conversation plays out most vividly through hands-on instruction in the Cary Collection, as, under your guidance, the GDA has actively supported design education. What a learning experience it has been, hosting your classes in our library. Your teaching collaborations with Kari Horowicz and Amelia Fontanel are always strong demonstrations of the power of inspiring and educating students through the use of primary materials. I also think of the summer master designer workshops held by you and Massimo Vignelli. Your students, up-and-coming and established graphic designers alike, would visit the Cary Collection during their lunch hours and other spare time to examine process material from the GDA. They, too, were joining the conversation you began.

Our own teaching collaborations centered mostly on class sessions presenting avant-garde typography and design. Here, too, is an example of your vision. You recognized that there was a gap that needed to be bridged between the Cary's historical collection of graphic communication material and the GDA's focus on modernist design. Working with you to identify exemplars of European avant-garde design from the early part of the 20th century, David Pankow and I have developed a significant collection that thematically ties together the Cary Collection and GDA.

The process of acquiring these various collections has taken us on many adventures, whether together, or on solo missions. You and I have held meetings in upscale design studios, hunted through a book remaindering warehouse in New Jersey, and, (I'm not sure if I told you about this one, but) I concluded a donor visit you arranged with a merry ukulele jam session over glasses of wine. Through your initiatives, we have met so many extraordinary people and learned so much about their lives and work. This has been a rich education unto itself and we thank you for it. You are always a generous and spirited companion.

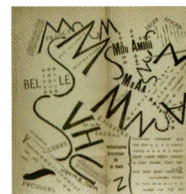

Above:
Lester Beall, poster sketches for the
Rural Electrification Administration, 1937
Photo by Juliana Culbert

Right:
Cipe Pineles, gouache sketch layout for
Glamour (November 1941)
Photo by Steven Galbraith

Opposite, left:
George Giusti, original art for the cover
for Holiday (April 1963)
Photo by Steven Galbraith

Opposite, right:
F. T. Marinetti, Les mots en liberté
futuristes (Milano: Edizioni futuriste di
"Poesia," 1919)
Photo by Amelia Fontanel

The Letter of the Day is R

Theresa Fitzgerald
Vice President Brand Creative
Sesame Workshop
Adjunct Professor, New York University
RIT, Communication Arts, Class of 1984

Respected. Renowned. Rigorous. Redefined. Research. Redesign. Refine. Repeat. Resilient. Remarkable. Revolutionary.

R. Roger Remington, Chair of the RIT Graphic Design department, is the driving force behind the dynamic design program and Vignelli Center. He, and a distinguished design faculty, introduced the process of rigorous exploration of modernist design movements. In the spirit of collaboration, our studio work demanded dedication to craft and extensive technical training. The practice was paired with design history, theory, and criticism to build a rationale around what makes a design good. We learned: design impacts everything. As a first-year student, I arrived as a decorator, with a passion for the elaborate. After four years, I left a designer, with a focus on the minimal.

With a passion for design and a spirit for play, I headed to New York City to follow my dreams to create design for kids. With diligence and good fortune, I have successfully influenced some of the world's most beloved entertainment brands, including Nickelodeon, National Geographic, Discovery Channel, Scholastic, Peanuts, Mattel, and Sesame Street. Generally speaking, the children's market it is not known for its sleek design. In many cases, children's mass-market design is a visual assault, littered with dancing typography, cluttered compositions, and rainbow sparkles. I wanted to change that. There was an opportunity to create, improve, and reshape design for children. I believe smart design ignites kids' imagination to explore and curiosity to play. Good design does not talk down to kids, but lifts them up to learn. Design should engage and delight, without needing silly gimmicks. And design impacts everything.

Across all platforms, including websites, books, toys, packaging, experiences, motion graphics, and games design, standards of excellence have been raised and communicated in brand books and style guides. At Nickelodeon, the fun-first brand, the design signature was kid modern, with a hint of mess. At Sesame Street, the social good education brand, simple playful expressions in minimal designs for preschool. Kids learn the alphabet with clean typography to celebrate letterforms and amplify meaning. Design impacts everything.

We are celebrating R. Roger Remington's design legacy, which has impacted millions of kids, around the world, to thrive. It has been my intention to share my education with kids to encourage, inspire, motivate, explore, and learn through good design. Thank you, R. Roger Remington.

Ode to a
Holistic
Practicioner

Timothy Samara
Designer, Author, Educator

Accomplish.
Archive.
Augment.

Contribute.
Chronicle.
Catalyze.

Develop.
Document.   Invent.
Demonstrate.   Inscribe.
                             Inspire.

Formulate.
Frame.   Model.
Facilitate.   Mediate.
                             Mentor.

                             Produce.
                             Preserve.
                             Propagate.

                             R.
                             Roger.
                             Remington.

According to Diderot...

THE TRIPLE THREAT

MAKER

HISTORIAN

TEACHER

3

Tom Ockerse
Designer, Educator
Rhode Island School of Design

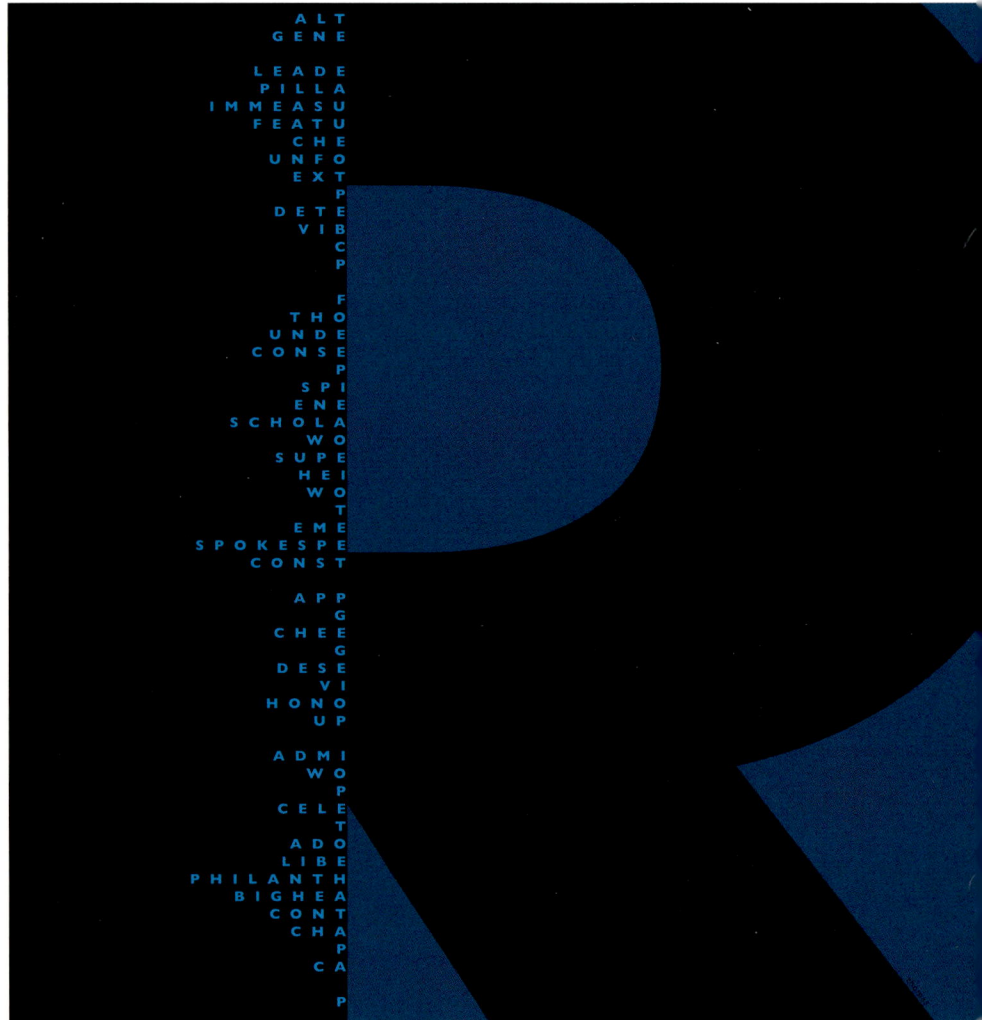

Design, Tom Ockerse, 2021

ALTRUISTIC
GENEROUS
RENOWNED
LEADER
PILLAR
IMMEASURABLE
FEATURED
CHERISHED
UNFORGETTABLE
EXTRA
PRESTIGIOUS
DETERMINED
VIBRANT
CRUCIAL
PRIME
REFINED
FRIEND
THOROUGH
UNDERSTANDING
CONSERVING
PROMINENT
SPIRITED
ENERGETIC
SCHOLARLY
WORLD-CLASS
SUPERB
HEIRLOOMED
WORSHIPPED
TRUSTED
EMERITUS
SPOKESPERSON
CONSTRUCTIVE
RECOGNIZED
APPRECIATED
GRACEFUL
CHEERED
GRACIOUS
DESERVING
VIRTUOUS

HONORABLE
UPRIGHT
RESPECTED
ADMIRED
WORTHY
PRAISED
CELEBRATED
TREASURED
ADORED
LIBERAL
PHILANTHROPIC
BIGHEARTED
CONTRIBUTING
CHARITABLE
PRECIOUS
CARING
RELIABLE
PRIZED

Four Female American Designers in the Cary Graphic Design Archive at RIT

Tom Strong
Designer, Author, Educator

Here are four of the ten twentieth-century American female designers whose work has been collected by Roger Remington. They are included in the Cary Graphic Design Archive.

This page:
Handkerchief chairs
Design by Lella and Massimo Vignelli,
Photo by Josh Owen

Opposite left top:
"Alphabet Series,"
Design by Elaine Lustig Cohen,
giclee print, 2007
Cary Graphic Design Archive

Opposite left bottom:
Elliot Carter album cover
Design by Henrietta Condak
paste up, c. 1970
Cary Graphic Design Archive

Opposite, right:
"When He Says 'Rain,' It Rains!"
illustration for Jack Stenbuck
Design by Cipe Pineles
Coronet, January 1947
Cary Graphic Design Archive

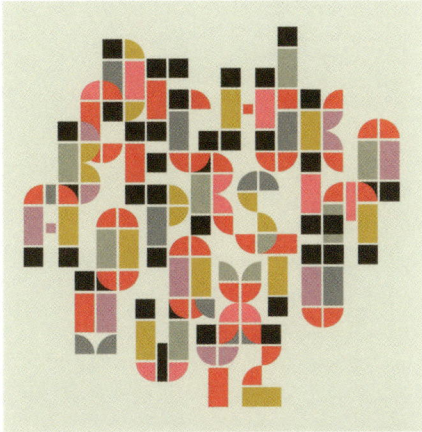

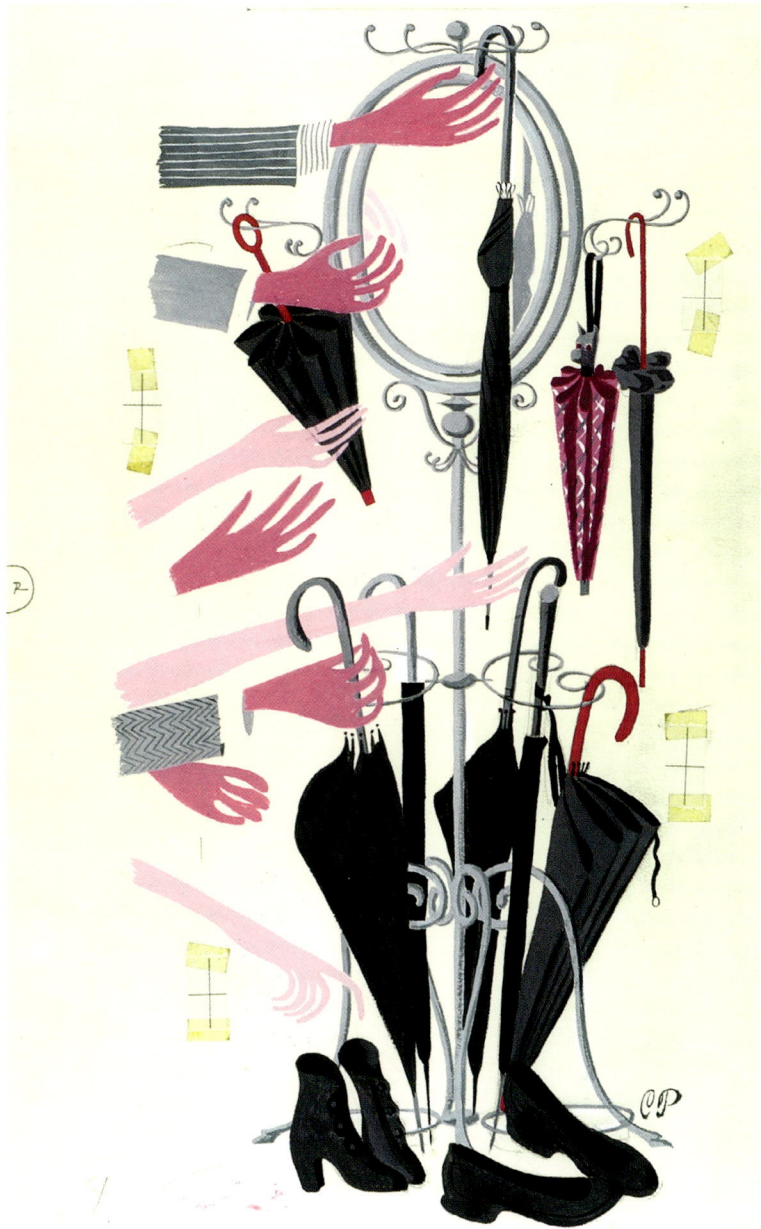

advocacy
noun
active support of a cause

Vignelli Center for Design Studies

Trista Finch
RIT Graduate, 2020
Vignelli Center Council Member
Designer

I first met Roger when I was a sophomore in Graphic Design at RIT, when I was chosen to become part of the Vignelli Council. Little did I know then how much of an impact working with and getting to know Roger, and everyone else on the Council, would have on me. His embodiment of *advocacy* was especially on display in the Council meetings. Every week you could always count on Roger having a table full of new and old books for us to read, posters or new acquisitions to the archive, articles he printed out to share with us, or updates about what his friends and colleagues were working on. He consistently encouraged the people around him, specifically the students, to surround themselves with design that goes beyond trends into the realm of the often quoted "Vignelli timelessness." Roger doesn't just give this great advice–he lives it. And his advocacy wasn't limited to advice about design. He was always encouraging us (the student representatives of the Vignelli Center)

to question everything, to bring first- and second-year students to the Council meetings, and to use the resources that RIT provided for us (many of which, like the Graphic Design Archive, in addition to the Vignelli Center, he had a hand in bringing to life, but he probably wouldn't tell you that).

If you didn't get the chance to see his office in the Vignelli Center, you missed out: the best view on campus with floor-to-ceiling windows on three sides, the fourth holding all of the books (and awards and mementos) you would expect a man like Roger to have, all surrounding Vignelli-designed furniture and objects. One of the ways I served on the Vignelli Council was by helping with the website and some print materials for upcoming events, which required a weekly meeting in his office to keep each other updated. At these meetings we got to know each other well, both professionally and personally

(to the point of questioning why my husband, known as Mr. Wonderful to Roger, didn't ask him for permission before proposing). Roger has helped me redesign my resume, we have worked through several typography projects together just for the fun of it (all the critiques of these projects are scribbled on new cut-and-pasted versions of the previous round, many of which I've kept to remind myself to come back to pencil and paper more often), and he has even helped me get a few jobs. Roger has been profoundly influential in my life, especially considering the relatively short time that I have known him.

This book is filled with past students, colleagues (many of whom used to be students), and other people who, at some point in their lives and careers, were the recipients of Roger's personal investment. He became an instant mentor of mine, which is something I will be proud to say for the rest of my life. I hope to continue to carry the torch that he and his legacy helped ignite.

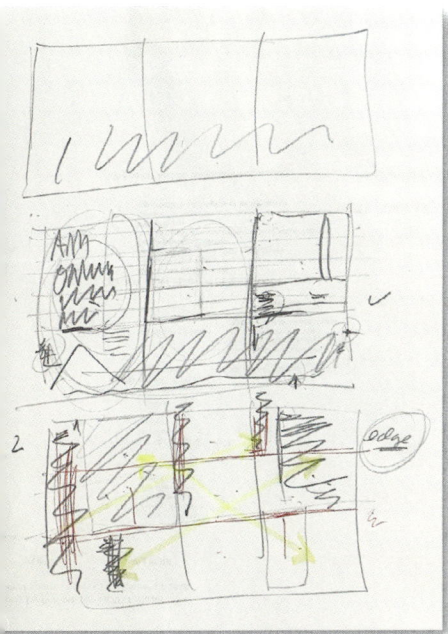

Opposite:
Trista Finch in front of the Vignelli Center for Design Studies
Photo by Elizabeth Lamark

Above, left:
Roger Remington's scribbled guidance for a poster project
Photo by Trista Finch

Above, right:
A corner of Roger Remington's office in the in the Vignelli Center for Design Studies featuring furniture designed by Massimo and Lella Vignelli
Photo by Trista Finch

A Summer of Design Lasts a Lifetime

Wendy Beth Jackelow, MFA, CMI, FAMI
RIT Graduate, Medical Illustration
Principal, Wendy Beth Jackelow
Medical & Scientific Illustration

In 1984, I was studying for an MFA in the medical illustration department at RIT, and I stayed on campus for the summer to work and take extra credits. I felt that my understanding of design was lacking, so I decided to immerse myself in a summer introduction to graphic design taught by Professor Roger Remington. From that course I gained several important things—a deeper understanding and appreciation of design, as well as two lifelong artist friends I never would have met if not for that class.

Before the rise of desktop design, all graphics were created manually. It is hard to imagine how it used to be, but lines were hand-ruled with a T-square and triangle, type was set by a typesetter, and layouts were pasted up with paper and glue. One measured with a ruler and used French curves and circle templates to render anything that was not a straight line. It required concentration, meticulous craftsmanship, and a very steady hand. It was in this environment that Professor Remington taught us the essentials of design.

That summer we learned step-by-step how to lay out a page. We constructed grids, identified and measured type, sized graphics, made thumbnails and mock-ups, and then pasted up a final piece. There were posters and calendars and booklets. We took information, both visual and written, and pieced it all together to make comprehensive visual solutions. Good design made sense to the audience and not just to the designer. It was artistry and organization mixed with logic, psychology, and practicality. The design should never overshadow the information. Roger taught all of this to us within the context of the history of design. Not only was he a skilled designer and teacher, but also an authority on design history. We worked hard, but the payoff of knowledge was immeasurable. We were being schooled by a master.

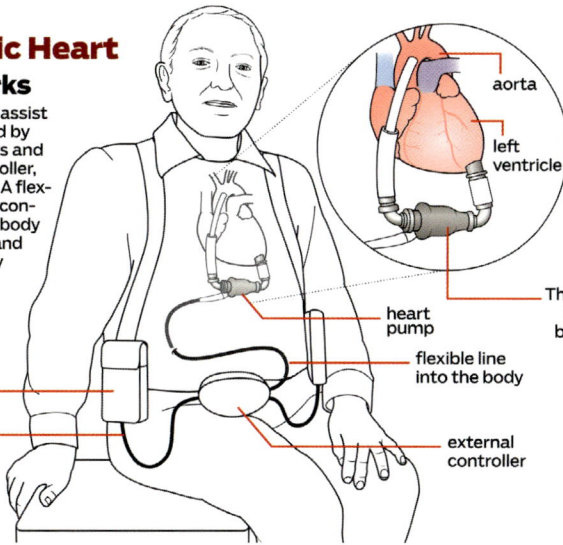

The Bionic Heart

How it works

The left ventricle assist device is powered by external batteries and an external controller, worn on the belt. A flexible line from the controller enters the body above the waist and connects directly to the pump.

battery holsters on both sides of body

power lines

aorta

left ventricle

Looking inside

The heart pump circulates the blood from the left ventricle to the aorta.

heart pump

flexible line into the body

external controller

The Bionic Heart
AARP *Bulletin*
Wendy Beth Jackelow, Illustrator

I know that many years have passed, but there is not a day that goes by when I do not consider and implement the lessons that were taught to me in Roger Remington's class. As a medical illustrator, I use those principles in every aspect of my illustration work—from adding labels to placement on the page. I consider the grid, the white space, the flow of the images, the typography, and the visual alignments. Everything I look at, I examine from a design standpoint, and it has made me a much better and more visually organized illustrator. I marvel at well-conceived graphics and shudder at those that fail. My way of thinking and observing everything visual—even the mundane—was completely altered by that summer class.

Roger Remington was my teacher at RIT, but he was something much more. He taught me how to think like an artist and designer. For this gift, I am truly grateful.

An Unparalleled Source

Wendy Marks
Director, University Gallery, RIT

R. Roger Remington is a colleague with an unparalleled source of ideas and information. He generously shares his wealth of personal and professional contacts from the world of design. He has curated numerous RIT University Gallery exhibitions that showcase accomplished and internationally recognized designers.

Roger Remington-curated exhibitions in University Gallery:

2011
Posters by Michael Bierut
*George Lois: Magazine Covers
and Advertising Design*
Bruno Monguzzi Posters

2012
Burton Kramer: Visual Music

2014
*Pierre Mendell: Posters from the Vignelli
Center for Design Studies*

2015
Musicians: Photographs by Bob Cato
*Milton Glaser: Posters from the Vignelli
Center for Design Studies*

2016
Ryszard Horowitz Photocomposer
*Norman Ives: Constructions and
Reconstructions*

2018
Another Side of R. Roger Remington
Master Drawings Lester Beall

2019
Abram Games
A Record of Britain's Social History
Steff Geissbuhler
Memorable and Imaginative Work

All images from Master Drawings
Lester Beall *exhibit, 2018*
Photos by Wendy Marks

Onward

R. Roger Remington
Graphic Designer, Educator
Historian, Author, Artist
Vignelli Distinguished Professor
of Design, Emeritus
Founding Director, Vignelli Center for
Design Studies, RIT

*"Age is an issue of mind over matter.
If you don't mind, it doesn't matter."*
MARK TWAIN

The Remington Family (most of them)

From my earliest years, I have always
had a life vision of bigger and better
things ahead in my future. One of my
heroes, Joseph Campbell, the scholar
who popularized mythology, used the
metaphor of experiencing life as a journey.
For him, the journey is important, yet
as the destination moves ahead, it is
apparent that the process of the journey
is important, not the ending place.

I view my fifty-seven years at RIT as
quite a voyage. Process, steadfastness
and confidence are the keys that have
unified the facets of my life, the tools by
which I have managed the constant of
change. On the subject of journeys,
Dr. Paul Miller, another one of my heroes,
who was RIT's sixth president between
1969 and 1979, said, "How journeys begin
and continue through twists in the road,
yield stories to be remembered and
perhaps told."

Hans Barschel

Roger Remington and Stanley Witmeyer

Bottom, right:
Roger Remington and Bruce Ian Meader

What follows is the brief telling of significant stories: the people, the events, the places, the process, and, of course my overarching attitude of persistence.

More than anything else, family has always been most important. From that center has come the wellspring of love and energy that has made all else possible. My life partners, my children Paula, Rob, and Leigh, and the grandkids Lindsey, Reed, Layne, Julia, and Rosemary... you are all life's blessing to me.

Sir Isaac Newton wrote, "If I have seen further, it is by standing on the shoulders of giants." This overused quote still has relevance as it has been my good fortune to relate with many important people:

· My teacher, colleague, and good friend the late Professor Hans Barschel, who opened my eyes to the world while I was such a naive student from a small town.

· My late teacher and colleague Professor Stanley Witmeyer, who was the model for an effective leader, teacher, and administrator with integrity and vision.

· My colleague and best friend Bruce Ian Meader, with whom I shared the importance of a formal aesthetic approach to making and teaching graphic design.

· My late colleague Rob Roy Kelly, who gave me a broad and uncompromising understanding of graphic design education.

Massimo Vignelli, Suzanne and Roger Remington

Rob Roy Kelly   Gene DePrez

Dr. Barbara Hodik   Dean Meeker

· My colleague Gene DePrez, who has kept alive the importance of the City of Rochester as a creative center of opportunity.

· My former colleague Dr. Barbara J. Hodik, with whom I coauthored my first book and shared international success with our legendary first conference on graphic design history.

· My late teacher, the artist Dean Meeker, who brought me to a new understanding of graphic form through his dynamic teaching.

· My colleague Anne Ghory-Goodman, with whom I shared the highlights of the first decade of the Vignelli Center for Design Studies.

· My colleague Josh Owen, with whom I shared a mutual love and respect for design function, simplicity, and elegance while expanding the Vignelli holdings.

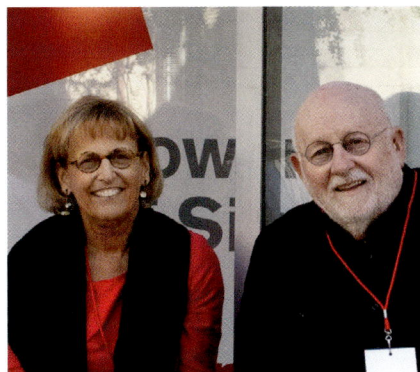

Anne Ghory-Goodman and Roger Remington

Josh Owen and Roger Remington

Joe Watson and Roger Remington
Photo courtesy Roger Remington

Massimo and Lella Vignelli at the
dedication of the Vignelli Center for
Design Studies, 16 September 2010

Opposite, top:
Roger Remington showing archived
Vignelli material in the Center's Hamlyn
Trust Study Room; Roger Remington
teaching in the Vignelli Center for Design
Studies; Jennifer Whitlock (5th from left)
and Vignelli Center staff preparing a
special presentation for visitors; Roger
Remington and his students at a 2013
summer design class in Venice, Italy
Photos these pages courtesy
Bruce Ian Meader

• My friend Joe Watson who was a key faculty colleague in the 1970s, our golden age of Graphic Design.

• My friends in England, Germany, Italy, France, Switzerland, Czech Republic, Sweden, Mexico, and Canada who have added such cultural breadth and richness to my life.

• My friends the late Massimo and Lella Vignelli who both supported my work, shared a great vision and taught me the importance of Modernism. It has been my great honor to extend their legacy.

• My students who have, in many ways, educated me, worked hard and then gone on to make great contributions to design and society.

Over the years, I have identified and brought to RIT many of the giants in the design world to lecture and do workshops. Exposing more than 200 such high achievers and pioneers to myself and my students has been a priority from which we all have benefitted.

As a product of RIT, it has been my good fortune to experience its growth from a small trade school to a major technological university (although I still prefer to call it the Institute.) I have found my way here through many open doors to achieve my goals and dreams.

One of my colleagues characterized me as, "Someone with an agenda" and I still view this as a compliment, indicating my vision forward. RIT has been the perfect base for my interests in teaching graphic design, developing archives, scholarly interpretation, and so much more. An important realization is that the Vignelli Center anchors design on the RIT campus and extends the Vignelli goals of education, preservation, collaboration, advocacy, and public good nationally and globally as well.

Having practiced in the field, I soon came to the conclusion that I much preferred working with people rather than producing things on paper. I estimate that I have worked with approximately 20,000 students. Of greatest importance in teaching graphic design, is an emphasis on the design process. In an educational environment that stresses the making of products, my interest has been in having my students think about the way in which they design and not necessarily rush ahead to an end product. Projects and products come and go, but the redeeming summative priority is the process. This is one aspect of the learning experience that students carry out into professional practice and it will be the one element that will sustain them throughout their careers.

My graduate studies at the University of Wisconsin-Madison were a critically important part of my creative development. I was fortunate to be there when the art school had an exceptional faculty. There I practiced graphic design, bolstered my understanding of art history and expanded into a new form language through printmaking. The seeds of my eventual move into teaching were sown at Wisconsin through teachers who were models of excellence. Here I learned that an outstanding school must have an outstanding faculty.

Additionally, I have always been on a search for learning opportunities. This has become a way of life and a means for unifying many of my interests. The connectedness of seemingly disparate ideas is a wonder. The threads of my own learning are exposed in each of the paragraphs above. My hope is that I have instilled this attitude in my students.

Framing these remembrances of my journey has been a rewarding experience. As I compose these thoughts, I continue to look ahead to new friends, achievements and adventures. The author John Abbate said, "When you embrace the journey rather than the end result, then process can become richer and more impactful, enjoyable and rewarding." What a journey!

Right:
R. Roger Remington at the Vignelli Center for Design Studies, 2012

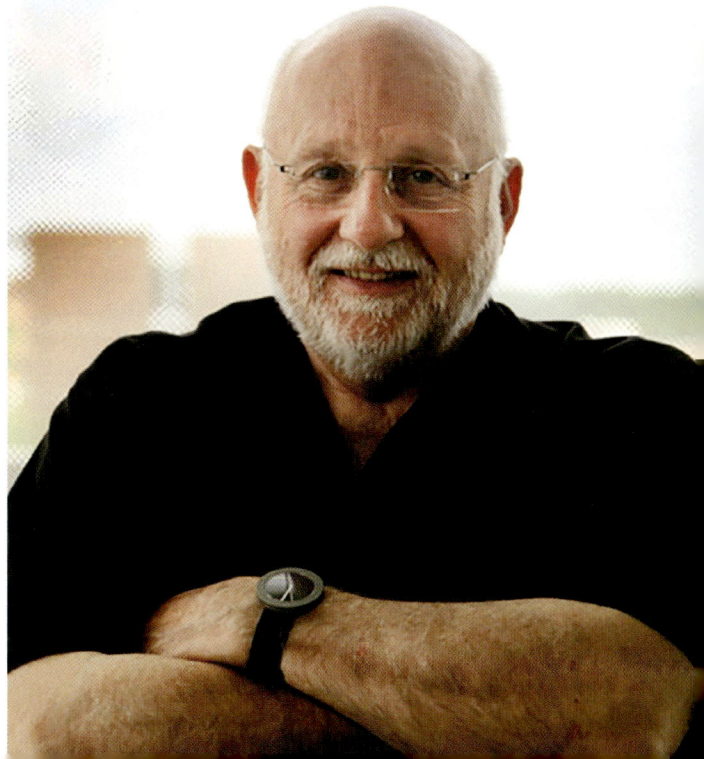

Special Thanks

Contributors

FRIENDS OF THE VIGNELLI CENTER
FOR DESIGN STUDIES

Design is One Believer
Chris Bailey
Design is One Aficionado
Sharon Napier
Design Devotee
Efecan and Peri Kababulut
Mark and Maura Resnick
Peter A Blacksburg
Reenie and Stanley Feingold
Design Champion
Daniel Skork
Doug and Margi Wadden
Gene and Patricia DePrez
Janice and Carey Corea
Joel Boches
Kristine Fitzgerald
Mark A. Daniels II
Design Enthusiast
Robert Appleton and Katharine Ishino
Steven Galbraith
Student of Design
Katharine Bassney

RIT HONORS COMMITTEE FOR
R. ROGER REMINGTON

Anne Ghory-Goodman
Professor Emerita
Milwaukee Institute of Art and Design
Visiting Scholar, RIT
Josh Owen, Committee Chair
Vignelli Distinguished Professor of Design
Director, Vignelli Center for
Design Studies, RIT
Katharine Bassney
Director of Advancement
College of Art and Design
College of Liberal Arts
RIT Library and Distinctive Collections
Lisa Vasaturo
Director of Alumni Relations
College of Art and Design, RIT
Peter Byrne
Director, School of Design, RIT
Steven Galbraith
Director, Cary Graphic Arts Archive, RIT
Todd Jokl
Dean, College of Art and Design, RIT

DESIGN AND
EDITORIAL TEAM

Anne Ghory-Goodman
Bruce Ian Meader
Jason Alger
Josh Owen
Steven Galbraith
Trista Finch

RIT PRESS

Bruce Austin
Director
Molly Cort
Managing Editor
Laura DiPonzio Heise
Business Manager
Marnie Soom
Design and Marketing Specialist
Amy Mantell
Copy Editor

Photo and Image Credits

Colophon

AUTHOR PHOTO CREDITS

p1 R. Roger Remington Archive; p4 Elizabeth Lamark; p8 Elizabeth Lamark; p10 Elizabeth Lamark; p12 Maria Bolivar Tucker, Elizabeth Lamark; p14 Michelle Shannon; p16 Elizabeth Lamark; p18 Celia McIntosh; p20 Armando Milani; p22 Deborah Bonnell; p24 Bruce Ian Meader; p26 Matteo Monguzzi; p28 Jeremy Kramer; p30 Lorrie Frear; p32 Todd Wolfe; p34 Esther Pulman; p36 MinJung Kim; p38 Mary Levine; p40 Norma Patiño; p42 Maya Tippett; p44 Global Innovation Partners; p46 Joy Bush; p48 Leslie dela Vega; p52 James Pienta; p56 Gail Fogarty; p58 Judy Infantino; p60 John Retallack; p62 Joe Watson; p64 Robert Lisak; p66 John Koegel; p68 Lulu Malinoski; p70 James Bogue; p72 Elizabeth Lamark; p74 Michael Brohm Photography; p76 Uwe Jacobshagen, Klaus Pollmeier; p78 Lee Green; p80 Elizabeth Lamark; p82 Caroline Pedrotti; p84 Chiara Pagani; p86 Adobe; p88 Michael Burke; p90 Bruce Miller; p92 Carole Woodlock; p94 Uwe Jacobshagen; p96 Alexander Skoirchet; p98 JuAnne Ng; p100 Marta Wojtal; p102 Annie Wolcott; p104 Sharon Poggenpohl; p106 Elizabeth Lamark; p108 Doug Keljikian; p110 Timothy Samara; p112 Tom Ockerse; p114 Tom Strong; p116 Elizabeth Lamark; p118 Laura Grace Marchi; p120 Elizabeth Lamark

IMAGE CREDITS

Unless otherwise credited, all images and photographs are used with the permission of the Cary Graphic Design Archives, the Cary Graphic Arts Collection, and the Vignelli Center for Design Studies at RIT.

Every reasonable effort has been made to contact the copyright holders of materials reproduced in this book.

TYPEFACES AND DESIGN

Neutraface 2, Text and Display is a typeface designed by Christian Schwartz, who had been influenced by the work of architect Richard Neutra. The typeface was chosen for its old style numerals and small capitals.

Neue Haas Grotesk Display, is a digital restoration of Max Miedinger's famous Swiss typeface Helvetica carefully redrawn by Christian Schwartz to match the original. This was Massimo Vignelli's favorite version of Helvetica.

Archetypal Vignelli design elements are visible throughout this book. The black rule above the author photos and the book's template reflect the modular Unigrid system Massimo Vignelli designed for the US National Park Service in 1977. The Vignelli Red endpapers give a nod to the Vignellis' studio identity.

The Final Word

R. Roger Remington,
Vignelli Professor
of Design, Emeritus
Founding Director, Vignelli Center
for Design Studies
In his RIT office, Room 4716, Level 4
Vignelli Center for Design Studies
April 2011
Photo courtesy Bruce Ian Meader